CANADA'S WORLD WAR II ACES

Heroic Pilots & Gunners of the Wartime Skies

Larry Gray

© 2006 by Folklore Publishing
First printed in 2006 10 9 8 7 6 5 4 3 2 1
Printed in Canada

The Publisher: Folklore Publishing
Website: www.folklorepublishing.com

Library and Archives Canada Cataloguing in Publication

Gray, Larry, 1937–
    Canada's World War II aces : heroic pilots & gunners of the wartime skies / Larry Gray.

Includes bibliographical references and index.
ISBN-13: 978-1-894864-58-9
ISBN-10: 1-894864-58-1

    1. Canada. Royal Canadian Air Force—Biography. 2. World War, 1939-1945—Aerial operations, Canadian. 3. Air pilots, Military—Canada—Biography. 4. Canadian. Royal Canadian Air Force—Biography. I. Title.

D792.C2G68 2006   940.54'4971'0922   C2006-901008-0

Project Director: Faye Boer
Project Editor: Bridget Stirling
Production: Linda Bolger, Willa Kung, HR Media
Cover Image: F/L John Alexander Kent. RE68-1625, Canadian Forces, National Defence. Reproduced with the permission of the Minister of Public Works and Government Services, 2006.
Photography credits: Every effort has been made to accurately credit the sources of photographs. Any errors or omissions should be directed to the publisher for changes in future editions. *Photographs courtesy of* Canadian Forces, National Defence, reproduced with the permission of the Minister of Public Works and Government Services, 2006 (title page, PL-41719; p. 10, PL-35524; p. 15, PL-41715; p. 22, PL-24137; p. 32–33, PL-33041; p. 39, PL-28865; p. 46, PL-19586; p. 54–55, PL-19744; p. 61, PL-22010; p. 67, PL-14179; p. 72, PL-31094; p. 93, PL-30466; p. 98, PL-35919; p. 115, PL-36581; p. 122, PL-28271; p. 130, PL-54000; p. 138–39, RE68-1625; p. 150–51, PL-8576; p. 155, PL-37034; p. 163, PL-43233; p. 169, PL-29398; p. 186, PL-21715); Don Sheppard (p. 104; p. 108); Air Force magazine (p. 84; p. 87).

We acknowledge the support of the Alberta Foundation for the Arts for our publishing program.

PC:PC5

Contents

❧❀❧

Acknowledgements

SINCERE THANKS TO MY EDITOR, BRIDGET STIRLING, FOR HER assiduous attention to detail and indulgence and empathy when a writer strays. I am very grateful to Hugh Halliday, who sets the Air Force historical standard and from whose book, *The Tumbling Sky*, I freely borrowed. Without Hugh's research help I never would have accomplished this. Thanks also to Robbie Hughes, for naval aviation information; Laurie Nyveen, for information on Canadians flying with the Israeli Air Force during the 1948 War of Independence; Claire Wilson, widow of Denny Wilson, John McElroy's wing mate; Janet LaCroix, Canadian Forces Photo Interpretation Unit; Don Sheppard for his information and provision of his photograph; Laurie Barnes of *Air Force* magazine, who helped determine whether or not these people have appeared in the "Last Post" column. Last but never least, to my wife, Gloria, who suffers the task of first edit and proof reading.

Introduction

THESE ARE STORIES OF ORDINARY CANADIANS DOING extraordinary things in extraordinary times.

The romantic notion of the World War I fighter pilot swirling and twisting in lofty blue skies, regarded as a knight of the air and last bastion of chivalry, was quickly dashed in World War II.

Wartime fighter pilots sought every possible benefit; it was a survival tactic. They climbed to height as quickly as was permitted and they treasured possession of an altitude advantage. The pilot's hope was to sight the enemy before he himself was sighted and use his slight advantage to gain a position between the enemy aircraft and the sun. Diving out of the sun, he was virtually invisible to his foe. He accelerated in the dive and positioned himself to attack the rear of the formation. Thus he hoped to avoid their defensive fire and maintain enough speed to carry out a successful attack on his first dive and still be able to maneuver away. If the attack failed, a dedicated professional fighter pilot used his speed to flee in order to fight another day rather than pursue an alerted enemy.

Young Canadian flyers were locked in battle with the German Luftwaffe as early as the autumn of 1939. In the late '30s, aspiring Canadian aviators paid for their own flying lessons and then bought

tickets across the Atlantic to join the British Royal
Air Force (RAF). It was the only game in town; the
Royal Canadian Air Force (RCAF) saw no need to
satisfy young Canadians' itch to fly. Moreover,
the government was not interested in equipping
the RCAF to meet an enemy force. So many
Canadians joined the RAF that a Canadian
squadron, No. 242, was formed in November
1939. Its commanding officer and all pilots were
CAN/RAF (Canadians serving in the RAF). Later
in the war, the Canadian government wanted
Canadian airmen to fly in Canadian squadrons.
Several Canadian squadrons were renumbered on
March 1, 1941 to the 400–449 series to differenti-
ate them from RAF Squadrons. Operational control
remained with RAF headquarters, and many
Canadian airmen achieved high rank and positions
of command within the RAF structure.

In 1939, the RCAF had 210 aircraft and planned
to enlarge its permanent force to 525 officers and
4500 other ranks. At the end of May 1945, serving
members totalled 164,846, and 11,239 of them
were women. At its peak in 1944, more than
215,000 members were on strength (officially serving with the RCAF). More than 95,000 had gone
overseas, and 50 percent of the aircrew had served
with the RAF. Hugh Halliday lists 154 Canadian
pilots who achieved the coveted ace status. Thirty-
six aces were killed in action, and a further seven
died in flying accidents.

The French air force first used the term "Ace" in 1915 to describe an airman who had destroyed five or more enemy aircraft. Both the American and German air forces adopted the practice, and both kept official lists of airmen's victories. The British and Commonwealth air forces did not adopt this practice, choosing not to give fighter pilots prominence over other airmen. No running tally of individual victories was kept, so air historians must scour individual and squadron records to determine each pilot's confirmed victories.

Researchers find it difficult to substantiate victories. Pilots' claims were made in good faith, but confirmation by intelligence officers required firm evidence. During hectic or prolonged aerial battles, the number of enemy aircraft reported destroyed often exceeded the number actually shot down. Combat had many variables, but historians must accept that fighter pilots exaggerated their success. Likewise, their combat reports must be taken as subjective, since later research has shown some claims were inaccurate, and there may be no evidence to support or deny the accounts.

Remember also that every fighter pilot's success in the air meant that another young man flying an airplane for his country plummeted to earth, trapped in the flaming fuselage of his aircraft. A downed pilot had little chance of survival.

This book introduces the reader to a few of the aircrew credited with sufficient victories to be called "ace". They are not all pilots, and they are not all the recognised leading scorers. They are simply young Canadian men who were lured by an ideal to put on a uniform and perform near-miracles in an alien and hostile environment.

Why did they go? Why did they stay?

These questions are somewhat answered in a letter written on September 22, 1940 by Pilot Officer W.C. McKnight to a friend in Calgary. McKnight was a CAN/RAF pilot who joined No. 242 Squadron in November 1939. By that time, he had over 700 hours in the air and won a Distinguished Flying Cross for his score of 16½ kills. McKnight wrote:

> *"Lady Luck must be a permanent passenger when I go up. I am still being offered a chance to return home as an instructor but the old reasons still keep me here, and I suppose I shall remain here until the end or until the other end. I've got used to the thrill and the, I don't know how to express it, final feeling of victory, that I'd be lost and bored by the quiet life again. This war business changes people a lot."*

McKnight would have been 22 years old 13 days after he disappeared from the maelstrom of air combat, declared missing, presumed dead on January 12, 1941.

Note: A glossary of terms can be found at the end of this book.

CHAPTER ONE

Richard J. "Dick" Audet
Cinq d'un Coup
(1922–1945)

IN DECEMBER 1944, FLIGHT LIEUTENANT RICHARD J. "DICK" Audet had been overseas for two years. Although Dick was flying with a front line Spitfire squadron, he had yet to fire his guns at an enemy target. Audet had spent most of his time either in training or as a tug aircraft pilot, but he had served a month with 421 Squadron, based at Kenley, Surrey, during the summer of 1943. There he flew four operational sorties, but no enemy aircraft sailed within the aiming circle of his guns. On September 14, 1944, he was posted to 411 Squadron, operating from a forward field near Brussels. Finally, Audet felt like he was at war.

Dick Audet was born on March 13, 1922, in Lethbridge, Alberta, the youngest of his Québecois parents' six children. His father's ranch was in the shadow of the Rocky Mountains near Coutts, and he was expected to do his share of chores. But he still had time for baseball, basketball, badminton and tennis, and the boy grew into a dark, handsome young man over six feet tall. Audet attended local schools and graduated from business college in

Flight Lieutenant Richard J. Audet, DFC

Lethbridge in the winter of 1941. The following summer he worked as a stenographer, but he heard the siren song of the air. On August 28, 1941, in Calgary, Richard Audet was sworn into the Royal Canadian Air Force.

The recruiting officer was so impressed with Richard's intelligence and personality that he recommended Richard be trained as a pilot. First, he had to be transformed into an airman. He was sent to No. 2 Manning Depot in Brandon, Manitoba, to learn the basics of air force service and become a credit to the uniform. While waiting for an opening in aircrew training, Dick worked as a guard at the Service Flight Training School in Brandon.

Dick's instruction in the intricacies of aviation began at No. 3 Initial Training School in Victoriaville, Québec, where he reported in February 1942. He then began pilot training at No. 22 Elementary Flight Training School in L'Ancienne-Lorette, outside Québec City. The postings in Québec gave him the opportunity to revisit his roots. His father, Paul, grew up in Baie-Saint-Paul, and his mother, Edewisca, in Coaticook. He began flying the Fleet Finch, a small biplane, then progressed to the Harvard at No. 2 Service Flying Training School, located at Uplands Airfield in Ottawa (the Macdonald-Cartier Ottawa International Airport now stands at Uplands). With each success, he was promoted, first to leading aircraftsman and then to sergeant. Prime Minister William Lyon Mackenzie King pinned a pilot's flying badge to Dick's chest on October 24, 1942. The young flyer was simultaneously commissioned to the rank of pilot officer. Richard Audet was on his way to the United Kingdom.

His first stop was the No. 3 Personnel Reception Centre in Bournemouth, England. After many weeks of waiting and five months of operational and advanced training, Audet was posted to 421 (RCAF) Squadron on July 20, 1943. After flying four sorties, he was posted back to Bournemouth, where he was sent to 691 (RAF) Squadron to fly a tug plane towing drogue targets for an anti-aircraft artillery unit. From December 1943 to July 1944, now promoted to Flying Officer, Dick Audet towed targets back and forth, chafing at the news of each Canadian fighter pilot's success. One bright spot occurred on July 9, when he wed Iris Christina Gibbons, a young English rose he had wooed for several months.

Following the wedding, Dick was posted to Kirton-on-Lindsey, where he spent a month honing his operational fighting skills before going to the continent and joining 411 Squadron at Evère, Belgium, on September 14. Combat still eluded him as he flew monotonous patrols over Allied lines. After battles over the Seine in August and over Nijmegen, Netherlands, in September, the Luftwaffe had disappeared from western skies, devoting their attention to the eastern front.

The squadron took up dive-bombing duties. Dick showed some flair for the task. On one occasion his section of three aircraft, flying as a unit, bombed a rail junction with total success. On another sortie, his bomb severed a railroad spur line and damaged a nearby factory. That summer, the squadron flew sweeps over the northern flank of the battle searching for German aircraft to engage and ground targets to bomb.

Following the rapidly advancing Allied ground forces, the squadron moved to Le Culot on September 21, Rips on October 4, Volkel on October 24—the day after Dick was promoted to flight lieutenant—and Heesch on December 6. Audet had flown 52 sorties up until December 29, but he had taken part in only three dogfights with still no opportunity to shoot.

On December 29, 1944, at noon, Oberleutnant Dortenmann led his 12th Staffel of 12 "Dora-9s" (Focke-Wulf 190D-9s) from their field at Varrelsbusch into battle against the Spitfires of 411 Squadron. They met west of Osnabruck.

Flight Lieutenant Richard J. Audet pushed the throttle of his Spitfire IXe forward and listened to the Merlin engine scream as it increased power. At 1256 hours, he released the brakes, and his machine shot down the runway. Audet was leading a group of four fighters called Yellow Section. On his right wing was Flying Officer D.F. Campbell (Yellow 2), and on his left flew Flying Officer J.M. McCauley (Yellow 3). Forming the fourth point of the diamond directly behind his leader was Flying Officer R.C. McCracken (Yellow 4). They climbed through the clear blue sky, cruising at 10,500 feet over the Rheine-Osnabruck area of Germany. Suddenly, Audet's headphones squawked with the voice of the radar controller reporting enemy aircraft at 10,000 feet at Rheine. Yellow Section turned to intercept.

They spotted one of the new German jet fighters, a Messerschmitt 262. At the same time, a gaggle of 12 enemy aircraft came into view. They were lower than the Canadians, flying slightly off to the right in line astern formation. The enemy group was four Messerschmitt 109s and eight Focke-Wulf 190s. The Canadians had the advantage of height and speed, and the section rolled out about 200 yards behind the trailing German. Audet opened fire, and strikes bloomed all over the enemy plane's fuse-lage and wing roots. When he broke off his attack, the German plane burst into flames on the right side and was trailing thick black smoke. Both of Audet's wingmen watched the aircraft go down in flames, crashing about six miles northwest of Osnabruck. Audet had his first kill.

He had descended to 8500 feet and was flying a defensive circle when he spotted a Focke-Wulf 190. Audet attacked, firing from 250 yards down to 100 yards as he closed on the enemy from behind, striking the aircraft over the cockpit and along the fuselage. The engine caught fire, and as Audet flew close over top, he saw the pilot slumped over in the seat. Flying Officer Campbell, Yellow 2, witnessed the fight and saw the enemy go down, cockpit flaming.

Immediately, Audet saw a Messerschmitt 109 and followed in a shallow dive. The enemy climbed

One of Canada's hottest fighter pilots, Dick Audet, with his Spitfire.

❧✦❧

sharply, and his canopy top flew off at 3500 feet. Dick fired a short burst from about 300 yards and saw "a black object on the edge of the cockpit, but his chute ripped to shreds." Apparently the pilot tried to bail out. Audet took photos of the aircraft crashing and breaking into flaming pieces on impact. Audet did not recall seeing any strikes on the airplane and thought he might have pressed only the "Browning button," which fired his machine guns (the Spitfire was armed with two 22-millimetre cannons and four Browning .303 machine guns).

Audet then spotted a Yellow Section Spitfire at about 5000 feet pursuing a Focke-Wulf 190. Another 190 was chasing the Spitfire. Dick radioed the other pilot to break, and he attacked the second Focke-Wulf from behind, following in a steep dive. Audet opened fire from 250 yards, striking the enemy along the length of the fuselage. The aircraft burst into flames and flew straight into the ground.

A few minutes later, Audet was trying to gather his section back into formation at 4000 feet when he saw one more Focke-Wulf 190 about 2000 feet below. Diving to attack, he saw the German fly towards him from the right and then swing left to attack Audet head-on. Dick eased back on the throttle, letting the enemy get into range of his guns. At about 200 yards he fired a short burst, and although he saw no strikes, the enemy plane flicked violently over and over until it hit the ground.

The "Green Hearts" of III/JG54 (3rd Gruppe, 54 Jagdgeschwader) suffered 14 pilots killed and at least 17 aircraft destroyed on December 29, their "Schwartzer Tag" (Black Day).

Dick's section was back on the ground at 1417 hours. In less than five minutes Audet had destroyed five German aircraft. With his wingmen's confirmation, he had become an ace on his first aerial combat sortie—an astonishing feat. Later, the pictures from his cameras proved his claims, and he was recommended for an immediate decoration.

On January 14, 1945, Dick was awarded the Distinguished Flying Cross:

> *"In a most spirited action, Flying Officer Audet* [his promotion had not reached everyone] *achieved outstanding success by destroying five enemy aircraft. This feat is a splendid tribute to his brilliant shooting, great gallantry, and tenacity."*

In the same encounter, McCracken, Audet's Yellow 4, also destroyed a Focke-Wulf 190 in an action witnessed by his leader. The squadron racked up two more kills, and that night they celebrated. Exhausted, Dick Audet, who did not drink, went to bed early.

Success begets success. The self-effacing Alberta boy strapped into a Spitfire cockpit became a confident, talented fighter pilot. On January 1, 1945, he destroyed two more Focke-Wulf 190s in the air near Twente. At the same time, the Luftwaffe was trying to wipe out the three RCAF bases at Evère, Heesch and Eindhoven with low-level bombing and strafing runs, resulting in heavy Canadian losses. Many airmen were killed and wounded, and many aircraft were destroyed or damaged sitting on the ground. Heesch suffered neither casualties nor damage, but the German pilots mauled Evère and Eindhoven.

On January 4, on patrol with Flight Lieutenant J.J. Boyle over the Hengels area, each pilot shot down a Focke-Wulf 190, and they shared the claim to a third. Once Dick had tasted action there was no stopping him. On January 14, another 190 spiraled to the earth, the victim of Audet's guns.

On January 22, he cheated death while on patrol near Osnabruck. A long-range fuel tank slung below his fuselage was hit by flak and exploded. The aircraft was severely damaged, but he managed to nurse it back to base. He was back in the air the next day, flying an armed reconnaissance sortie in the Lingen-Munster area. Over the Rheine airfield, the base for most of the Luftwaffe's operational Messerchmitt 262s, Dick noticed aircraft parked in a line on the west side. Lining up on them, he dove to strafe the stationary machines. A tractor began pulling one aircraft towards the edge of the airfield. Audet aimed slightly ahead of the tractor, and at 100 yards, cut loose with his guns. The target ran into his stream of bullets, and the 262 burst into flames.

On the way home, he saw a Messerschmitt 262 approach Rheine, preparing to land. Audet dove from 8000 feet to 4500 feet. The German saw him coming and raised his wheels to gain speed, but the jet was slow and Audet had built up tremendous speed in his dive. At close range, Audet triggered his guns. The Messerschmitt caught fire, hit the ground and exploded. Dick had set an incredible record. In 27 days, December 29 to January 24, he had destroyed 10½ enemy aircraft in air-to-air combat and one more on the ground. No RCAF or RAF pilot has ever equaled this feat.

On January 24, near Munster, he damaged a Messerschmitt 262, but this time the German got away. Targets became scarce as the Luftwaffe concentrated most of its resources on the Silesian battlefield on the eastern front. But not all the danger came from enemy pilots. Flak was an ever-present threat. On February 8, while attacking an enemy airfield, Audet's aircraft was hit, and the controls were severely damaged. He managed to get home to Heesch but could not level the airplane properly. The plane was too dangerous to land, so Audet climbed to a reasonable altitude and bailed out.

Soon afterwards he went on leave to England for a short visit with Iris. He was back in the fray on March 2.

On March 9, the *London Gazette* announced Audet's award of a bar for his Distinguished Flying Cross:

> *"This officer is an outstanding fighter. Since his first engagement, towards the end of December 1944, he has completed numerous sorties during which he has destroyed a further six enemy aircraft, bringing his total victories to 11. Flight Lieutenant Audet has also most effectively attacked locomotives and mechanical vehicles. His skill and daring have won the highest praise."*

Richard Audet never saw the citation for this second award. The day after his return from leave, on March 3, 1945, he was attacking a train on a rail siding near Munster, an especially dangerous mission since most trains had heavily armed flak cars attached. He was at 500 feet on a bombing and strafing run when anti-aircraft fire hit the Spitfire, and the plane burst into flames. At just 23 years old, Dick Audet died in the crash near the town of Coesfeld.

In the Squadron Operations Book, his mates wrote his epitaph:

"Modest and unassuming, he was just one of the boys and a real credit to Canada and her RCAF. His daring and keenness led to his presumed death. He was a leader, respected and admired by all. Just one swell guy."

After the war, Audet's body could not be found. His name is inscribed on the Commonwealth Air Forces Memorial at Runnymede, England, "For those who have no known grave."

CHAPTER TWO

Russell "Russ" Bannock
In the Rocket's Red Glare
(1919–)

IN 1984, RUSSELL BANNOCK WAS INDUCTED INTO THE Canadian Aviation Hall of Fame. His citation read, "His inspiring leadership as an instructor and fighter pilot in World War II, his unusual skills as a test pilot, and his corporate business leadership have all been of outstanding benefit to Canadian aviation."

Russell's contribution to the Royal Canadian Air Force and to aviation lore in Canada was all this and more, with one exception. He was not a fighter pilot in the traditional sense, a single pilot in a single-engine machine. Russ Bannock's combat operations were spent in the cockpits of twin-engine Mosquitos, flying with a navigator on intruder sorties.

As the war progressed, intruder squadrons were formed to fly patrols into hostile air space to destroy enemy aircraft on the ground, landing or departing from their home bases. Intruders were usually lone wolves but often flew flower patrols with other Mosquitos, supporting bomber raids or attacking the enemy's night-fighter bases. As the Luftwaffe departed for other fronts and largely left the western skies to Allied aircraft, the intruders flew ranger operations. These flights occurred day

Squadron Leader Russell Bannock, DFC and Bar, on course in
Greenwood in 1944.

or night against any target: trains, ships, vehicles,
military installations or aircraft. The sorties were
planned to achieve maximum surprise and hit
crowded areas. The task of the intruder was to
attack where he was least likely to be found.

Russ Bannock and his navigators were one of
Canada's most successful night intruder crews.

Their final total was nine aircraft destroyed in the air, two on the ground and nineteen V-1 buzz bombs intercepted and destroyed.

∽◆∾

Russell was born to Austrian immigrants William and Julia (Jarman) Bahnuk on November 1, 1919. His father was a construction foreman for the Grand Trunk Pacific Railway, which was later absorbed by Canadian National Railways. Russell and his older brother, Albert, spent their childhood in the town of Cooking Lake, Alberta. The boys trapped muskrats for their skins and, by age 12, Russell became a skilled duck hunter using a single-barreled shotgun. The brothers attended Eastwood High School in Edmonton from 1932 to 1936. The city's airport, Blatchford Field, hosted almost every famous bush pilot of the time—figures as well known and admired then as the fictional super-heroes of today. Russell caught the flying bug and spent many hours at the municipal airport or at the Cooking Lake seaplane base, dreaming of becoming a master of the skies. He built model airplanes and learned the flight characteristics of each one.

On graduating from high school in 1937, Russell, ever the adventurer, took a job as a freight purser and night bar steward on board the SS *Distributor*, a Hudson's Bay Company (HBC) ship that plied the waters of the Northwest Territories to the Arctic Ocean. The following summer, Bannock was swinging a sledgehammer for Consolidated Mining and

Smelting at their Golden Lake gold mines. He earned sufficient money to fund flying lessons at the Northern Alberta Aero Club while he took a mineralogy course from January to March 1938. He then went back to mining, swinging a sledge in Moberly Lake, BC, saving enough cash to continue his flying lessons. In the summer of 1939, Russell became the proud owner of a commercial pilot's licence. Yukon Southern Air Transport hired him to fly as second pilot on the route from Edmonton to Fort St. John.

In September 1939, Russ was invited by the Royal Canadian Air Force to fly as a provisional pilot officer. He took a two-month course in instrument flying at the Vancouver Flying Club and then rode the transcontinental train to Trenton, Ontario, for a one-month officer training course. He was just 20 years old, but Bannock already had considerable twin-engine flying experience. Moving on to Camp Borden, Russell trained on Harvards, Fairey Battles and Ansons as a member of the first wartime pilots' course. He won his air force wings, graduating from Wartime Course No. 1 on February 28, 1940. Russell's enlistment in the RCAF contrasted with his two cousins who were serving in the German Luftwaffe.

Because of Austria's participation with Germany in the war after the invasion in March 1938, William Bahnuk found it politically appropriate to anglicize his family's surname to "Bannock." The change became official on February 20, 1940.

Canadian troops were stalled in England by the fall
of France and Hitler's domination of Europe. Russell's
flight training was put to good use because the
expanding British Commonwealth Air Training Plan
needed trained pilots to teach new flyers. Instead of
going overseas, Russell taught at Trenton and then
No. 3 Central Flying School in Arnprior, Ontario. From
1940 to 1943 he chafed in his role as a teacher but
rose quickly through the officer ranks, becoming
a squadron leader on November 1, 1942. Finally,
in December 1943, Bannock was sent to No. 36
Operational Training Unit in Greenwood, Nova Scotia,
where he met his Scottish-born navigator, Robert Roy
Bruce. The two quickly became a formidable team
in the fast and beautiful de Havilland Mosquito.

Bannock and Bruce sailed for England and
joined No. 418 Squadron, the RCAF's only intruder
squadron, at Holmsley South airbase on June 10,
1944. The squadron's crest displayed an Inuit standing on an ice flow holding a harpoon. The "Eskimo"
squadron bore the motto *Piyautailili,* an Inuit word
meaning "defend even unto death." They had blanket clearance to roam from the fjords of Norway to
the Mediterranean and attack any target of opportunity in between. Sorties varied from making
lightning-quick strikes against railway yards and
military installations to dropping money and supplies to the French Maquis (resistance fighters).

When the Germans started firing V-1 and V-2
rockets at Britain, 418 Squadron was assigned to

intercept them. On their first operational flight, on the night of June 14–15, Bannock and Bruce racked up their first score. They were flying a night intruder sortie to the enemy airfield at Avord, 100 miles south of Paris. The team's first successful sortie almost became their last.

Approaching the airfield, Bannock picked up the tail light of an aircraft making its final approach to land. He started to follow it, but the ground defenders, knowing a Mosquito was nearby, turned on a searchlight and opened fire with their anti-aircraft batteries. Bannock had to break off his pursuit, but as he did, the enemy aircraft turned on its landing lights. Turning towards him, Bannock opened fire and was rewarded with a brilliant explosion. It was light enough for the Mosquito crew to identify a Messerschmitt 110.

Surrounded by a solid wall of flak, he kicked his aircraft into a tight right turn—so sharp that at 300 miles per hour the airplane did a sudden roll. Bannock pulled it into a high-speed stall, and it rolled just as he was caught in the searchlights. His instructing experience saved him as he instinctively let go of the stick. He could see the trees below him, but his Mosquito shuddered and righted itself, and he stayed within the deadly wall of flak. Both he and Bruce shook all the way home.

About this time, the squadron adopted the name "City of Edmonton." To celebrate and to announce the new name to the Germans, bricks wrapped in the *Edmonton Journal* were dropped during a subsequent raid.

In June, the team also saw their first pilotless bomb heading for England. It looked like a burning aircraft traveling at high speed. When Bannock reported the sighting to his radio controller, he was told he had just seen the exhaust of a V-1 pulse jet engine. Shortly afterward, 418 Squadron began anti-diver patrols, intercepting the new threat at night. A V-1 shot down over England could still kill and maim people on the ground; one shot down at sea could do no damage. The Mosquito had no radar, so the crews had to rely on the "Mark I eyeball"—their own vision—to hunt and destroy buzz bombs.

Although fast, the Mosquito could not cruise at more than 400 miles per hour, the speed needed to catch and overtake the flying bombs. Russ Bannock and Don MacFadyen, a friend from his instructing days, devised a different tactic, patrolling the French coast at 10,000 feet while watching for the telltale flames of the pulse jet exhaust. They followed the V-1 across the Channel. At halfway, they commenced a high-speed dive that allowed the aircraft to reach a speed of 440 miles per hour, closing on the bomb and providing a brief opportunity to shoot to kill. MacFadyen and his navigator got the first V-1 on the night of June 16–17. Bannock and Bruce got their first V-1, the squadron's second, on the night of June 19–20.

The crew got three of the five they attacked on the night of July 3–4, and they set a record for the

RCAF and the RAF with four more kills on the night
of July 6–7. By the end of July, they had shot down
another eight. During August, they destroyed three
more to make a total of 19. They also learned that
it was a good idea to close one eye on the attack
run. That way, they would retain their night vision
in the closed eye following the blinding flash of the
bomb's explosion. Their last successful attack on
a buzz bomb was on the night of August 12–13.
After hitting their target, they watched in amaze-
ment as the V-1 slowed and wavered. Its autopilot
turned it back towards France, where it crashed and
exploded near Boulogne.

Air intruder operations were not ignored. In
mid-July, they flew a sortie deep into the Reich to
Altenberg, south of Leipzig. Intelligence reports
indicated that the Luftwaffe was training pilots for
night fighting there. When the team arrived, they
destroyed one Focke-Wulf 190 and damaged
another, both in the air, before heavy flak drove
them off. Bannock was given command of B Flight
in July, and he and Bruce were both awarded
Distinguished Flying Crosses.

On August 30, they participated in a ranger attack
on the Vaerlose airfield near Copenhagen. Swooping in at treetop level, they set one Junkers 88 on
fire with a short burst then spotted a Messerschmitt
110 with a mechanic working near its tail. Bannock
reported: "After one look at us he broke all speed
records during a sprint in an easterly direction."

Another burst set the parked Messerschmitt on fire, and the Mosquitos headed home.

On September 27, Bannock and Bruce flew the sortie that would add bars to their Distinguished Flying Crosses. The Luftwaffe had an operational training unit on the Baltic Sea, just south of Berlin, an obvious target with many enemy aircraft. The base was far enough from Britain to lull the training German pilots into a sense of security. Russ Bannock wanted to damage that feeling of comfort and planned a solo daylight ranger sortie. In hindsight, he acknowledged that it would have been a safer trip had he taken another Mosquito with him.

Bannock and Bruce left Hunsdon at 0400 hours and flew over the Continent in pitch-black skies. When they arrived over the enemy airfield, they found 8 to 10 training aircraft already airborne in the circuit. The German air force used as a trainer the four-seater Messerschmitt 108—equivalent to the Harvard used by the RCAF. Swooping in on the unsuspecting pilots, Bannock quickly lined up a plane in his sights and shot it down. Another aircraft quickly came into view, and it too met the same fate. Not satisfied, Bannock continued circling, trying to set his sights on a Bucker Jungmeister biplane. The Mosquito crew should have been prudent and left, having lost the element of surprise.

"Russ, we have an Me 109 shooting at us!" shouted Bob Bruce from the navigator's seat. To lighten the plane, Bannock immediately dropped his 100-gallon external fuel tanks, which were almost empty, and the Mosquito shot forward. The German pilot was flying an older model of the Messerschmitt, and he was easily out-maneuvered by the Canadian, but not before the Mosquito took two hits in the left wing. Diving to the treetops, Bannock turned west. Suddenly, the port engine burst into flames. By reflex, Bannock feathered the propeller and hit the left fire extinguisher button. The crew was still deep in northern Germany with only one engine. And instead of the forecast cloud cover that would have provided hiding places for the crippled aircraft, Bannock and Bruce were flying through beautiful blue skies in bright sunshine.

Bruce suggested, "The only way we are getting home is if we head for Sweden." Russ didn't think much of that idea. He had no intention of spending the rest of the war interned in neutral Sweden. Skimming the waves of the Baltic, they crossed southern Denmark, dodging a couple of Junkers 88 transports that were oblivious to their passing. Bannock was tempted to line up and fire on them, but he realized that would be tempting fate just a little too much. With only one engine running and the pilot reducing the fuel flow mixture, they crossed the North Sea. Inbound aircraft usually landed at Coltishaw for refueling, but Bannock overflew the airstrip and landed, 7 hours and 15 minutes after taking off, at Hunsdon.

Later that afternoon, the squadron engineering officer found Bannock over coffee in the officers' mess and showed him a piece of Perspex about the size of a thumbnail from one of the Messerschmitt 108s the crew had shot down. The fragment had penetrated their radiator. The loss of coolant had caused the engine fire, not bullets from the Messerschmitt 109. The external radiators on the bottom of the Mosquito's engines were especially vulnerable to debris from smashed targets.

In mid-October, Bannock was promoted to wing commander and took command of 418 Squadron, which was starting to strike ground targets. In November, he was transferred to the command of 406 Squadron, a night-fighter squadron that had just been reassigned to intruder duty, taking the place of 418 Squadron. He and a few other 418 pilots were expected to train the 406 flyers in intruder tactics. The squadron was equipped with new Mark 30 Mosquitos with the Mark X airborne intercept radar. When Bannock arrived on November 23, No. 406 Squadron was moving to Manston aerodrome. Bannock teamed up with a new navigator, Flight Lieutenant Clarence J. "Kirk" Kirkpatrick of Kindersley, Saskatchewan. The new commanding officer proved he could fly a desk as well as an aircraft, and 406 flourished as a new intruder squadron under his command. Russ brought Bob Bruce to 406 as squadron navigator to hone the map reading and dead-reckoning skills that were the intruder navigator's forte.

The most successful Mosquito crew of 418 Squadron, Russ
Bannock (left) and Bob Bruce, at the nose of their aircraft.

On Christmas Eve, 1944, the 406 Operations Record Book noted that the squadron sent six intruder sorties into Germany and the Netherlands. Bannock and Kirkpatrick, flying Mosquito *MM693*, took off at 1715 hours. At 2225 they landed, completing a successful flower operation. They were briefed to go to Gutersloh aerodrome and arrived at 1920 hours. Since there was no activity there, they set course for Paderborn. The airfield was lit up with its red outer perimeter lights and a single flare path with the outer and inner horizon bars illuminated. The rotating beacon was flashing. All these lights told the attackers that aircraft were either coming home or taking off. Visibility was excellent in a clear sky with bright moonlight.

Lurking in the circuit, they spotted a Junkers 88 flying 3000 feet ahead. After a series of circling maneuvers, the Canadians got to within 200 feet, slightly below the enemy aircraft. It was flying at 150 miles per hour, wheels down, ready to land. The crew gave it a one-and-a-half-second burst. Immediately, the port engine exploded, and the port wing caught fire. The doomed aircraft spiraled down and crashed about three miles from the aerodrome, spreading debris over a 100-foot area.

Squadron members were elated at their first intruder victory under their new commanding officer. Christmas Day dawned bright and fine. While the squadron flew two operational flights to the Netherlands, the officers still had time to visit the Airmen's Mess and the WAAF quarters in Westgate to serve Christmas dinner and beer, as was the custom in the air force. The Record Book noted: "No Christmas entertainment whatsoever was planned by the station and those off-duty celebrated the festive day individually."

January 1, 1945, was a cloudy day, and the conditions got no better that night. However, Bannock and Kirkpatrick brought back the happy news that they had destroyed a Heinkel 111 that was taxiing on the ground at a field in southern Denmark.

The pair's last victory together was on the night of April 23–24. They were patrolling near Wittstock when the airfield lighting started to flash, warning aircraft in the circuit of the intruder's presence. The team saw a Junkers 88 crash while trying a low approach to avoid their Mosquito. Later, at 0310 hours, they made contact with another Junkers 88 that twisted and turned in violent evasive action. Sticking with the bomber, the Mosquito avoided the top gunner's red tracer fire and struck along the enemy's fuselage and starboard engine. A parachute sailed past their windscreen. The third burst from Bannock's guns caused the enemy plane to catch fire and crash into nearby woods.

Bannock qualified for his Operations Wings on July 20, 1945. This little golden wing, worn on the left breast pocket over the letter O, indicated that a pilot had completed at least one tour of operations, usually 30 to 33 sorties.

When Wing Commander Russell Bannock's war ended, he was the premier intruder ace of the RCAF. In recognition of his bravery in the air and his leadership on the ground, Russell Bannock was awarded the Distinguished Service Order on August 17, 1945. The citation noted that he was largely responsible for 406 Squadron's efficiency and success in its transition from night fighter to intruder operations:

"As a squadron commander, Wing Commander Bannock has proved to be an outstanding success. Since the award of the Distinguished Flying Cross, he has destroyed a further seven enemy aircraft, bringing his total victories to at least 11 enemy aircraft destroyed and others damaged. He has also destroyed 19 flying bombs by night. In addition, he caused considerable disruption of the enemy's lines of communications. Under this officer's inspiring leadership, his squadron has obtained a fine record of successes and reached a high standard of operational efficiency."

The final score for Bannock and his navigators was nine aircraft destroyed in the air, two aircraft destroyed on the ground, four aircraft damaged in the air, 19 flying bombs destroyed, four locomotives damaged and 11 motor vehicles destroyed or damaged.

With the cessation of hostilities, Bannock was sent to the RAF Staff College for the war staff course. He completed the training in December 1945 and was appointed the first postwar air attaché to Moscow. Before he was able to take up his post, fate intervened. Geoffrey de Havilland offered Russell a job as chief test pilot for the company that built his beloved Mosquito. Bannock said yes and became the first to take De Havilland's famous Beaver off the ground. The Beaver was the first aircraft designed for short takeoffs and landings (STOL). He was also a test pilot on the Twin Otter and the first De Havilland jet fighter, the Vampire. Russell became vice president in charge of sales before he left the company in 1968 to form his own consulting firm, Bannock Aerospace Limited.

In 1975 Russell returned to De Havilland, and the next year he was appointed president and CEO. In April 1984, he was inducted into the Canadian Aviation Hall of Fame. He flew his own Beaver aircraft for 22 years until, at age 84, he gave up flying and sold the plane in April 2004.

Russell remained in contact with his first navigator, Bob Bruce, who was a skilled pianist and composer. Bruce became a professor of music at Cardiff University. In 1970, he delivered a special composition to his former pilot. The *Bannock-Bruce Symphony*, an original work based upon their experiences in 418 Squadron, has been played by several symphonies and was recorded by the Warsaw Symphony Orchestra.

CHAPTER THREE

Robert Carl "Moose" Fumerton
Eyes That See In the Dark
(1913–)

FLYING OFFICER ROBERT CARL FUMERTON REPORTED TO 406 Squadron, based at Acklington on England's east coast, on June 20, 1941. A brash young Canadian, at 28 he was considered elderly by the rest of the squadron pilots. Although he had extensive flying experience, he had little familiarity with combat. He soon adapted to life as one of Sir Winston Churchill's "few."

Fumerton arrived in England in August 1940 to join No. 112 Squadron, one of the RCAF's first contributions to the defence of Britain. The army cooperation unit flew clumsy, obsolete Lysanders. To his relief, on September 15, he went to a fighter operational training unit to train on the Hawker Hurricane. Fumerton then spent two months with No. 32 (RAF) Squadron flying from Biggin Hill and completed nine sorties. On November 29, he was transferred to No. 1 (RCAF) Squadron.

The Hurricane had provided stellar service to the RAF during the Battle of Britain, but with the Luftwaffe's introduction of the Messerschmitt Bf 109E in 1941, the Hurricane was totally outclassed.

Wing Commander Robert Carl Fumerton, DFC and Bar.

The new and exciting Spitfire soon replaced the Hurricane as the primary RAF fighter.

As the Battle of Britain was winding down, the Canadian squadron was flying Hurricanes from Prestwick, Scotland. Although the Luftwaffe continued to raid Britain, it was licking its wounds and reorganizing. Fumerton built up a considerable number of flying hours but still had not made contact with the enemy. At Acklington, Northumberland, No. 406 (Lynx) Squadron became the first RCAF night-fighter squadron. Pilots teamed up with navigators to form combat crews. Sergeant L.P.S. "Pat" Bing of Regina became Fumerton's partner. They trained on twin-engine Blenheims until the squadron was equipped with the formidable Beaufighters.

Fumerton and Bing were on patrol in aircraft *J*, 10,000 feet over Acklington, on September 1. They waited for ground radar controllers to vector them towards any approaching German aircraft. The controller had a target and sent them racing off to the northwest through the black British skies. Soon Bing picked up the target on his radar, and although his equipment was acting up, he directed his pilot closer. Over Bedlington, a dark bomber came into view about 1500 feet above them. Fumerton followed the plane in and out of the clouds until it could be clearly seen against the moon. The crew identified the shape as a Junkers 88 and closed in for the kill.

Just as they had done hundreds of times in training, Bing kept his eye on the bogey on his scope while Fumerton let the Beaufighter drop until they were below and behind their prey. At close range, Fumerton opened fire with the four 20-millimetre cannons in the nose and the six .303 machine guns. Strikes flashed on the Junkers' fuselage, and its right engine burst into flames. The bomber fell to the left and Fumerton followed even as the enemy gunner returned fire. The shots went wide of the Beaufighter, and Fumerton lined up his target from behind and fired again. A brilliant flash lit up the night as the bomber exploded.

Two hours and 10 minutes after they had taken off, Fumerton and Bing landed at Acklington. They had scored their first victory, the first ever for an RCAF night fighter and 406 Squadron's first success. The next morning, the men of 406 found the wreckage and cut out the black Iron Cross insignia of the Luftwaffe, taking it back to base (the insignia is now on display in the Canadian War Museum). None of the German crew survived, so the officers of 406 Squadron provided a full military funeral.

Robert Carl Fumerton was born in the village of Fort-Coulonge, Québec. In the 1700s, French soldiers had built a log fort where the Coulonge River emptied into the Ottawa. The fort became a gateway to the Pontiac region and a haven for coureurs de bois from the sometimes-hostile Iroquois.

The son of George and Katherine (Parr) Fumerton, Robert grew to a lanky six feet. He was very much at home living off the land, hunting and fishing in the forest south of Pembroke. At school, the muscular youth played hockey, football and softball. He earned his junior matriculation at Shawville in 1930.

At 18, he left school and found a job in the woods as a timber cruiser for a lumber company. Next, he worked for International Nickel, and then, in 1934, Fumerton went into prospecting with the eminent geologist Dr. Joseph Retty who discovered iron ore in Labrador. Throughout the Depression years of 1935–9, he prospected with various exploration companies in northern Ontario and the Northwest Territories. Somewhere along the way, he acquired the nickname "Moose," which stayed with him for the rest of his life.

Moose took correspondence courses in geology and surveying and was interested in aerial photography related to mapping. He began flying at the Sudbury Flying Club, earning his private pilot's licence in the summer of 1939.

With the advent of war, Moose left the woods for Ottawa, where he joined the Royal Canadian Air Force on November 6, 1939. He was sent to Lakehead Flying Club in Fort William (now Thunder Bay) for further flying experience. On March 24, 1940, Moose went to the flight training school in Camp Borden to learn to fly Harvards. On May 20, Air Marshall "Billy" Bishop, the renowned fighter ace from World War I, pinned air force wings to Fumerton's tunic.

Carl "Moose" Fumerton received his commission as a pilot officer, and after one summer in Ottawa, proceeded to England where he began flying with No. 112 Army Cooperation Squadron. He was promoted to flying officer on July 13.

A week after their initial success, Fumerton and Bing encountered and damaged a Heinkel 111.

That sortie was their last trip over Britain with 406 Squadron.

On October 19, 1941 the team was sent to No. 89 (RAF) Squadron. Originally a World War I training squadron, No. 89 had reformed just three weeks earlier at Colerne as a night-fighter unit, flying Bristol Beaufighters. In November, the squadron moved to Abu Sueir in Egypt. Just after Fumerton and Bing joined No. 89, on November 15, 1941, Moose was promoted to flight lieutenant. Moose and Bing arrived in the Middle East on Christmas Day and flew their first night patrol on January 5, 1942.

In the early morning darkness of March 3, the four Beaufighters on alert scrambled to intercept incoming enemy aircraft. In the light of the bright moon, they saw a Heinkel 111 cruising above the Suez Canal. The Allied planes turned to attack and opened fire as they rapidly closed on the bomber. The vigilant German rear gunner returned a deadly stream of bullets that destroyed Fumerton's gunsight and hit his right leg just above the ankle. Debris from the reflective sight cut him around his right eye and cheek. His right engine also took hits and began to lose power.

Nonetheless, Moose turned the Beaufighter in for a second pass, correcting his aim by the red streaks from his tracer bullets. Both engines on the Heinkel burned as it dove and crashed into the sea. Fumerton's second engine quit, and he and Pat prepared to ditch into the Nile Delta. At about

200 feet, one of the engines caught and roared back to life. However, the speed was so low that Moose could only fly directly ahead. With unusable flaps and a damaged undercarriage, he was forced to make a wheels-up landing at the aerodrome on Egypt's Edku salt flats.

The German crew escaped in a rubber raft and drifted for two days before an Allied rescue boat captured them. Fumerton spent a few restless days in hospital before getting back into the air. In recognition of his "skillful flying, offensive spirit and endurance," Moose was awarded the Distinguished Flying Cross.

On the night of April 7–8, they scored again. Over the city of Alexandria, at the northern mouth of the Suez Canal, they attacked a Heinkel 111 and watched as the crew bailed out of the flaming aircraft before it crashed into the water. Moments later another Heinkel 111 blazed into the ground when a wing broke off. The team's score reached five, officially earning ace status.

Six crews and five aircraft, equipped with the new Mk IV airborne intercept radar, established C Flight of 89 Squadron at Luqa, Malta, on June 22. Bing was commissioned as a pilot officer. Under the constant attacks of the Luftwaffe, Allied pilots either destroyed enemy planes or were shot down. During their second night on the island, Fumerton and Bing destroyed a Junkers 87 and a Junkers 88. Over the next 10 nights, they shot down five more, all Junkers 88s. The crew's actions were rewarded with a bar to the Distinguished Flying Cross for Fumerton and the Distinguished Flying Cross for Bing. They destroyed two more planes while on Malta service—an Italian Z1007 on August 14 and another Junkers 88 on August 28.

All of this success was not without cost. On the night of August 10–11, they were scrambled in aircraft *7748* to intercept raiders incoming from Sicily. It was a muggy night, with strong winds causing rolling waves in the Mediterranean. They were at 10,000 feet, closing in for the attack, when the starboard engine quit with a loud bang. Fumerton hit the propeller-feathering button. Suddenly, there was silence in the cockpit except for the whistling wind—the other engine had also failed. The Beaufighter was a poor glider, and within minutes the two men were dumped into the sea, standing on the airplane's wing trying to inflate their dinghies. Bing's raft was split, so the two clambered into one five-foot dinghy as the fighter sank. Bing had kept his helmet, which was mounted with a small battery-operated light. They were picked up by a rescue launch from Kalafrana and later learned that one of their own squadron Beaufighter pilots had spotted Pat's light and directed the boat to them.

On September 23, the crew flew back to Abu Sueir. Over the next two months, they were engaged in routine patrols and non-operational

Moose Fumerton commands No. 406 night-fighter squadron in England.

～oᲯᲪᲪᲪ～

flying. Moose Fumerton was promoted to squadron leader on October 1, 1942.

In December, the crew was posted home to Canada for Christmas. The two of them had a circuitous route by air to Florida and then by train to Montréal and Ottawa. Moose then took the train through Aylmer to Fort-Coulonge. It was a bittersweet return. His mother had died years before, and his father had remarried. But while he was en route between England and Egypt in November 1941, his father had died. His stepmother, Anne, was alone to welcome him home to Fort-Coulonge.

After his Christmas leave, Moose went to No. 1 Operational Training Unit in Bagotville, Québec, where he languished, with an interval at RAF Ferry Command. On July 18, 1943, he boarded an aircraft at Dorval to return to England. Back in a cockpit, he revived his love of flying and night-fighting skills. On August 25, he was promoted to wing commander and took command of 406 Squadron, where he had begun his combat career.

No. 406 was based at Anglesey in northern Wales and had not seen any action for months. The squadron was flying the older model Beaufighter, and morale was at an all-time low. Fumerton persuaded Fighter Command to move 406 to Exeter, Devon, closer to the air action, and he elicited a promise from Command to replace the Beaufighters with Mosquito XIIs. But the Mosquitos remained on the horizon, unavailable until the first machine was delivered in April 1944. Meanwhile, the Luftwaffe mounted major raids primarily on London, which left 406 too far away to be part of the action until the night of March 19. The Germans attacked the city of Hull, and 406 launched three Beaufighters to retaliate. Squadron Leader "Blackie" Williams shot down a Heinkel 177, giving the squadron its first victory in a year.

Fumerton was flying one of the new Mosquitos during a squadron scramble the night of May 14–15, 1944. After his hours on the Beaufighters, Moose found the smaller, lighter Mosquito a real pleasure to fly. The aircraft had responsive controls and was quick, nimble and fully aerobatic. Moose was cruising at 17,000 feet when the controller directed him toward an incoming Junkers 188. The German pilot spotted his pursuer and took violent evasive action. The Mosquito had no problem catching up to its prey. Fumerton let loose a long burst at about 100 yards. The Junkers' left engine exploded, and the plane went into a smoking dive to the sea. Moose Fumerton had just scored his 14th, and last, air-to-air victory.

Most of the RAF fighter controllers were British WAAFs (Woman's Auxiliary Air Force). Pilots learned to identify a particular voice that they heard often, just as the controllers got to know the pilots, especially the Commonwealth aviators with their strange accents. One female voice particularly intrigued Moose Fumerton. He sought her out, began a storybook romance and then married Flight Officer Madeleine Reay.

After D-Day, for which Fumerton delivered the operation order to Allied headquarters in southwest England, 406 Squadron settled in to flying patrols over the English Channel and providing air cover to Allied destroyers on coastal operations off Brest. Under Fumerton's leadership, the squadron destroyed 17 German aircraft. The No. 406 pilots stood down from active operations to trade in their Beaufighters and train on the potent new Mosquito Mark XXX.

The squadron learned that Fumerton was posted away in July. An unusual editorial appeared in the squadron's newsletter dated July 28, 1944:

> *"By far the most important and depressing news this week is the posting of Winco "Moose" Fullerton… It seems a mighty poor show to us all that such a good gang should be broken up by the posting of the chief organizer. Something had to be done and most definitely is being done, as we all know. The outcome of our efforts is yet to be seen, but at least we have made known our feelings in no uncertain terms."*

In the Royal Air Force, criticism of senior air officers was unthinkable, particularly in print. But considering the number of brash young Canadians in the squadron, with their well-known disdain for protocol, such a strong reaction was predictable.

Moose Fumerton returned to Canada to take command of No. 7 Operational Training Unit in Debert, Nova Scotia, until July 1945, when he took his release from the air force. He was awarded one final honour, the Air Force Cross, for his performance in his last command:

> *"…he very effectively reorganized discipline and flying training to the present high standard of efficiency. Through his personal and strong example he raised morale to unprecedented levels. At no time*

*of the day did this officer hesitate in offering his serv-
ices, and it is directly to this attitude that valuable
crews and aircraft were saved from destruction..."*

When Moose arrived in Ottawa for his release
proceedings in August, he was met at the train by
a *Citizen* reporter who revealed that Fumerton's
promotion to group captain had been announced
to the newspaper. It was the first Moose knew of
his new rank.

Moose and his war bride settled into quiet
Canadian civilian life—for a while. In 1948, Russ
Bannock, now with De Havilland, recruited a group
of Mosquito pilots, including Moose, to go to
China to train Nationalist Chinese (Kuomintang)
airmen. The nationalist Chinese had bought some
300 mothballed Mosquitos. The Canadians travelled to Hankow to find the training facilities in
extreme disarray. The Communists were closing
in, and early in 1949, the Canadians could do
nothing but pack up and go home.

Moose and Madeleine settled in Toronto, where
he became a real estate broker. Together they
raised four daughters, Gail, Maureen, Debbie and
Pattie, and one son, Richard.

CHAPTER FOUR

William T. "Bill" Klersy
Mors Celerrima Hostibus
(1922–1945)

AS LONG AS HE COULD REMEMBER, BILL KLERSY WANTED TO be a pilot. Born in Brantford, Ontario, on July 30, 1922, the son of William and Grace Klersy, he grew up in Toronto. He couldn't recall a specific incident that piqued his interest in flight, but he dreamed of becoming a bush pilot, flying alone into Canada's wilderness. To make the fantasy a reality, he took flying lessons at the Toronto Island Flying Club. Any money he made working summer jobs he spent on flying.

Canada went to war, and Bill read reports in the newspapers of famous bush pilots enlisting in the air force. He knew from talk at the flying club that the Royal Canadian Air Force had called upon anyone with a private pilot's licence to join up. Although he was an indifferent student, he completed high school. Immediately, on June 28, 1941, he presented himself to the Toronto recruiting unit. Klersy enlisted for pilot training as an aircraftsman second class and stayed in Toronto, learning air force rules and regulations at No. 1 Manning Depot, and then shifted to No. 6 Initial Training

School until December 5, 1941. Upon graduation, he was promoted to leading aircraftsman.

After Christmas leave at home, Bill went to Oshawa to No. 20 Elementary Flying Training School to begin two months flight training on Tiger Moths. His flying education continued on Yales and Harvards until June 19, 1942. At No. 6 Service Flight Training School in Dunnville, Ontario, Bill Klersy was presented with his winged flying badge and simultaneously commissioned as a pilot officer in the Royal Canadian Air Force. At last, he realized his dream of becoming a fighter pilot. But he wasn't going to see any action quite yet.

Klersy's first fighter squadron was No. 130 (Panther) Squadron at Mont-Joli, Québec, with Eastern Air Command. Until October 1942, the young pilots flew Curtis Kittyhawks. Then they converted to Mark XII Hurricanes. Mont-Joli was also the home of No. 9 Bombing and Gunnery School, so No. 130 Squadron fliers had to avoid becoming the targets of the gunners in their Fairey Battles. Klersy shared top target shooting honours with another Toronto pilot, and he and a fellow flyer set a record for "scrambling" to their aircraft in just 65 seconds. The achievement was not recognized, however, when trainers discovered that the two knew of the exercise in advance and were poised inside the ready room waiting for the warning bells to ring. Bill was establishing his willingness to push the envelope early in his career.

From May until June 22, 1943, Klersy waited at Y Depot in Halifax for a ship to take him overseas. He arrived in England on July 1, 1943, and reported as a supernumerary pilot to 401 (Ram) Squadron on July 9. The motto of 401 was *Mors Celerrima Hostibus* (Latin for "very swift death for the enemy"), and its badge was a Rocky Mountain bighorn sheep's head. The squadron was flying Spitfire Vs out of Redhill, Surrey, and escorting USAAF (United States Army Air Force) Mitchells on bombing raids to targets on the outskirts of the Luftwaffe's usual patrol areas. Consequently, they had little opportunity for airborne combat.

Klersy had plenty of flying time to hone his skills in navigation, target practice and formation flying with the squadron's veterans of Battle of Britain dogfights. Many of these pilots wore medals attesting to their bravery and skill, and they told the novice fighters their stories of flying against some of the best of the Luftwaffe.

In October, the squadron moved to Biggin Hill, where they were re-equipped with the superior Spitfire IXs. Bill Klersy finally put his training into practice and fired his guns at the enemy for the first time in late November. On an escort mission, his section strafed a German airbase at Cambrai, tangling with Focke-Wulf 190s of JG66's 2nd Gruppen. The section destroyed two 190s, and both German pilots were killed. On December 19, Bill was promoted to flying officer.

Flying Officer William T. Klersy (back row, third from the left) with 401 Squadron in 1943.

On Christmas Day, flying stopped at 1045 hours, and the squadron officers gathered in the sergeants' mess for drinks before going to the airmen's mess to serve the men's traditional Christmas dinner. That afternoon Klersy, now nicknamed "Gristle" (ostensibly due to his unruly curly hair), and Flight Lieutenant Jack Sheppard stole a Christmas tree from the station's main mess to adorn the wing mess (the wing included 401, 411 and 412 Squadrons).

The drinks flowed freely, and by the time the airmen had their dinner, most were feeling no pain. Klersy commandeered the tannoy (intercom) and taunted 411 and 412 Squadrons by announcing they were deadbeats waiting for a new supply of bows and arrows. They held a dance that night, but Klersy had "become unconscious" and was not back on his feet for several hours.

In 1944, the Russians relentlessly drove the German forces west. The Allied armies, including the 1st Canadian Division, advanced slowly north up Italy's boot. On January 9, Klersy and Pilot Officer "Tex" Davenport, of Windsor, Ontario, took off on a low-level attack on rocket gun emplacements. Their target was inland from Le Tourquet. About 25 miles after they crossed the French coast, Davenport's aircraft was hit by flak. The two pilots climbed into the clouds. Davenport then reported that his engine had quit, and he was going down. Klersy had no option but to return to base alone. Davenport was captured, but he escaped and was back at the squadron by mid-April.

On January 24, Yellow Section, led by Jack Sheppard and including Flying Officer Hayward, Flight Lieutenant Haywood and Klersy, took off in fair weather at 0915 hours to cover a short-range attack by 54 USAAF Marauders on the Le Tréport-Poix-Amiens area. On the way home, halfway between Boulogne and Dungeness, Sheppard's aircraft, with its only engine dead and no radio, began to lose altitude. The other pilots followed him down, and at 2800 feet, they saw him bail out. Klersy and Hayward circled over the site to direct the rescuers, but Klersy ran low on fuel and headed for land. He intercepted the Walrus rescue plane and led it back to Sheppard. Bill then flew to the nearest base, Hawkinge, and landed with only two gallons of fuel left in his tanks. Sheppard was saved from the waves by an air-sea rescue launch and taken to Hawkinge—the sea was too rough for the Walrus to set down.

Still, contact with the enemy eluded Bill Klersy. The routine of flying sweeps, escorts and patrols went on, but having no contact with any German opposition frustrated him. Then, on March 7, he got his chance. He was flying as Yellow Three with Jack Sheppard again, escorting 100 Marauders bombing a railroad marshalling area in France. North of Beaumont-sur-Oise, Sheppard saw a Focke-Wulf 190 at treetop level and led Yellow Section in a descent. Sheppard shot the enemy aircraft down with a single burst from his cannons. As they were climbing back up, Klersy spotted another 190 "on the deck" (just above the ground) and went down after it. He fired several good bursts into the engine and cockpit, and the enemy airplane half-rolled in flames and slammed into the ground. Klersy's first kill ended in a spectacular fireball on a hillside.

On April 1, the squadron had a first-class "thrash" at the nearby White Hart pub. "Gristle" Klersy pulled off another performance, capturing a chicken in the backyard, climbing back in through a window and triumphantly parading the squawking bird through the lounge. He was establishing a reputation as a party animal. Fortunately, the weather was too bad the following day for any flying.

On April 10, they all flew to Fairwood Common in Wales for gunnery, bombing and strafing practice, then they deployed to Tangmere and lived in tents preparing for the invasion of France.

In anticipation of D-Day, the squadron was busy softening as many of the German defences as they could. They were attached to 126 Wing of the 2nd Tactical Air Force and flew many hours on patrols, sweeps and dive-bombing runs. On May 20, the squadron went on a ranger operation near Cambrai. Opposition was light, so the pilots made low passes over the Vimy Memorial. For most of the men, it was their first look at this great tribute to the Canadian soldiers of World War I. They were awestruck by the monument shining against the dark horizon.

The early morning of D-Day, June 6, 1944, was cold, with scattered showers and low cumulus cloud. Klersy flew three sorties over the beachhead. As daylight waned, the city of Caen could clearly be seen burning in the distance.

June 7 was a very different day. The Luftwaffe, virtually absent from the skies on D-Day, rose to meet 401 Squadron's attackers. On the second patrol of the day, Klersy destroyed a Focke-Wulf 190 in a one-on-one dogfight. On June 10, 401 was the first squadron of No. 127 Wing to land in France for refueling. They and their ground crews moved to airstrip B-4 at Beny-sur-Mer on June 18. The men started out in tents but soon learned how to dig slit trenches as refuge from enemy attacks. German aircraft began appearing in strength, and flying debris from spent flak and bombs tore holes in the tents' canvas.

The summer of 1944 was eventful for Bill Klersy. On June 19, he received another promotion to flight lieutenant and his score began to mount. On June 28, 12 Focke-Wulf 190s bounced the squadron, and Klersy took down two of them. On July 2, he destroyed a Messerschmitt 109 east of Caen, and on the 13th, he damaged a Focke-Wulf 190 southeast of the city. On July 17, the section was on a dusk patrol northwest of Caen when they surprised three Dornier 217 bombers. The Canadians shot down two and damaged the third. Klersy was credited with one of the destroyed aircraft. On July 31, over Domfront, they attacked 12 Focke-Wulf 190s. Klersy picked off one, and it crashed in flames. His score was now seven destroyed and one damaged.

Klersy went on leave from August 17–29 and when he returned, he learned that he had been awarded the Distinguished Flying Cross:

> *"This officer has displayed the greatest keenness for operations. He has participated in a large number of sorties, on many of which he has led the flight with distinction. He is a most determined fighter and has shot down three enemy aircraft."*

This citation must have been written around the end of June.

On his return, Bill was given command of A Flight. Most of the air battles moved away from Caen as the ground forces pushed towards the Netherlands. The squadron pilots spent their time shooting up fleeing enemy vehicles. They were also making rapid moves, through Cristot, Evreux, St. André and Poix in France, reaching Brussels, Belgium, by September 7.

On September 16, Bill Klersy completed his 260-flying-hour tour and was sent to No. 83 Group Support Unit in England for a rest.

Around noon on October 2, the 1st Gruppe of JG26 sprang a trap on a section of 401 Squadron Spitfires. The Canadians had bounced a few Focke-Wulf 190s north of Nijmegen. The rest of

A typical fighter pilot activity while waiting to be scrambled. Bill Klersy is the curly-haired pilot on the right wearing his Mae West.

the Germans, hiding higher in the sky, fell on them and shot down two Canadian aircraft.

On October 23, 401 Squadron learned that Klersy and two others had received bars to their Distinguished Flying Crosses. The squadron flew 36 sorties on Christmas Day. The new commanding officer, Squadron Leader Hedley Everard, who had only taken command on November 24, bailed out south of Venlo and was taken prisoner. On January 3, 1945, Bill Klersy was made acting squadron leader and returned to the Continent to command 401 Squadron.

Klersy led his squadron into the air on a patrol that took them over Osnabruck on January 23. Just north of the town was an aerodrome with a number of jet aircraft taking off and landing. Unable to pass up such a golden opportunity, the squadron peeled off and attacked in waves, destroying three and damaging six enemy planes. After studying the pictures next day, they found that the enemy aircraft were a new type, the Ar-234, which was the fastest jet aircraft to fly during World War II. The planes they shot down were the four-engine bomber model, nicknamed "Blitz."

On March 1, the squadron flew only one sortie, on an armed reconnaissance mission in tandem with 412 Squadron. They were bounced by 40 Messerschmitt 109s and Focke-Wulf 190s. In the ensuing melee Klersy destroyed two Messerschmitts and a Focke-Wulf. He sent both 109s crashing to the ground in flames and then hit the 190 from astern. It spun into the ground and exploded. Klersy's score stood at 10 enemy aircraft destroyed.

Bad weather prevented most flying in early April, and those that did get airborne flew uneventful patrols. Many notations in the squadron diary asked: "Where are the Jerries?" Once again the Luftwaffe had vanished from the skies. By then, all but the youngest and most naive of the Jagdgeschwader pilots realized that the war was lost. On April 12, the Canadian squadron moved into Germany, to Rheine, and then on to Wunstorf on the 15th. Most of their action involved shooting up trains and road transport ahead of the Allied armies.

Leading a patrol over the Elbe River on April 19, Klersy spotted a lone Focke-Wulf 190. He closed in and destroyed it. The next day, 401 Squadron pilots destroyed 18 enemy aircraft and damaged six more. Klersy got 1½ Messerschmitt 109s over Schwerin in the afternoon—the half was a shared victory with his wingman—and in the evening, on patrol over Hagenau aerodrome, he accounted for two Focke-Wulf 190s.

The ground forces crossed the Elbe and 401 Squadron's pilots flew patrols over the bridgehead. On May 3, they were over Hamburg as the ground troops entered the city. Northwest of Kiel, they found a large number of enemy aircraft sitting on a grass strip. With no opposition from flak gunners, they were able to leisurely strafe the stationary planes until all their ammunition was expended. The total was 12 Junkers 52s, two Heinkel 111s and a single Junkers 87. Klersy was credited with one Junkers 52 and a Heinkel.

On May 8, the pilots and ground crew gathered around every available radio to hear Prime Minister Winston Churchill announce the official surrender of Germany. The squadron's celebrations consisted mainly of organizing sporting activities and relaxing in the sun.

But May 22 was a dreadful day for the squadron. Squadron Leader W.T. Klersy, the commanding officer, was reported missing on a training trip. He was leading two other Spitfires to a reunion of 401 pilots at the Savoy Hotel in London. Over the Rhine Valley, they ran into cloud, and Klersy radioed the others to climb. The other pilots saw him make a fast turn, but when the group of aircraft flew out of the cloud, there was no sign of Klersy. On the 25th, news arrived that his burned body had been found in the aircraft, crashed into a hill near Wesel. He had been at war for less than two years, had shot down and destroyed 16½ aircraft and damaged another 3½ and was still two months short of his 23rd birthday. He is buried in the Groesbeek Canadian War Cemetery near Nijmegen. On June 29, his award of the Distinguished Service Order was announced:

"Throughout two tours of operational duty, [Squadron Leader] Klersy has displayed outstanding leadership, courage and devotion to duty. Since the award of a bar to the Distinguished Flying Cross he has destroyed or damaged a further 90 enemy vehicles, eight locomotives and eight goods trucks. He has also destroyed three more enemy aircraft, bringing his total to at least 10 enemy aircraft destroyed. This officer has moulded his squadron into a powerful operational unit that, by maintaining a consistently high standard in every phase of ground or air activity, has set a magnificent example to the rest of the wing."

CHAPTER FIVE

John F. McElroy
From Militia Volunteer to Mahal Pilot
(1920–)

JOHN FREDERICK MCELROY ENDED HIS FLYING AND FIGHTING career with an impressive tally of 13½ enemy aircraft destroyed, eight of those while flying on RAF squadrons and the rest when on RCAF squadrons. He is also attributed with 2½ aircraft probably destroyed and nine damaged, and he had four Spitfires shot out from under him. After World War II, he flew and fought for Israel in the 1948 War of Independence and scored three more victories over the desert.

John McElroy joined the Royal Canadian Air Force immediately after graduating from Kamloops High School in June 1940. His father was a railroader with Canadian National Railways, and the family moved fairly often. John was born in Port Arthur, Ontario (now part of Thunder Bay), on November 3, 1920. Before Kamloops, the family lived in Vancouver and North Battleford. While in Saskatchewan, John joined the local militia regiment, the 16th/22nd Saskatchewan Horse (later known as the Battleford Light Infantry), and when he moved to British Columbia, he transferred to the Rocky Mountain Rangers. When he wasn't soldiering, he worked as a clerk and a labourer.

The recruiting officer who accepted young McElroy for training was impressed with his eagerness to serve. He was considered a typical fighter pilot. After indoctrination at the Manning Depot, John began flight training at No. 3 Initial Training School in Victoriaville, Québec. He passed the basic course and went to elementary flight training school. Although he had difficulty controlling the aircraft in spins and sideslips, he was still fighter pilot material and went on to Summerside, PEI, to attend No. 9 Service Flight Training School.

September 1, 1941, was a warm summer day on the Island. The graduating class paraded on the hangar line to be inspected and receive their pilot's flying badge. It was an especially auspicious day for John McElroy, who sported a new officer's uniform. As one of the top student flyers, he earned his commission as a pilot officer.

After some leave, McElroy sailed from Halifax for Britain. He waited at the Personnel Reception Centre in Bournemouth for a place on an operational training unit. Finally, in March 1942, he arrived in Castletown to fly Spitfires with No. 54 (RAF) Squadron. In early 1942, the squadron began carrying out coastal patrols.

In May, John and a squadron mate were flying a low-level exercise out over the water. Low cloud and haze obscured the horizon, and the new pilot

Flight Lieutenant John F. McElroy, DFC

was having difficulty judging his altitude. His baro-
metric altimeter was not accurate flying in the
variable pressure systems over the ocean, so his
instruments weren't much help. Abruptly, John's
Spitfire convulsed, and a spray of salt water splashed
across his windscreen—his propeller had touched
the water. His immediate reaction was to climb.

When he reached 7000 feet and leveled off, the plane was vibrating violently. His prop was bent, causing the aircraft to shudder. Shaken and chagrined, Pilot Officer McElroy nursed his airplane to the nearest airfield at Wick where he landed safely.

No. 54 Squadron was warned they would be transferred to Australia for duty in the Pacific, but in June, John McElroy was posted to join No. 249 Squadron in Malta. There, the squadron formed part of the fighter defences and flew fighter-bomber sorties over Sicily.

John made an inauspicious arrival. On June 9, he and George Beurling, another Canadian air ace, flew Spitfire VCs off the British aircraft carrier *Eagle* to land in Malta. McElroy had damaged his plane's tail on takeoff, and it crashed on landing. The unimpressed wing commander temporarily grounded him. On July 2, John had his first successful air combat and was credited with a damaged Messerschmitt 109. On July 10, he was doubly successful, destroying another 109 and an Italian Macchi MC 202 Folgore. By month's end, he claimed 5½ enemies destroyed, 1½ probably destroyed, and 4 damaged. McElroy had achieved ace status.

He flew many sorties in August and September, but he didn't bag another aircraft until September 29, when he shot down a Messerschmitt 109. October was a busy month as the Luftwaffe tried one last time to defeat Malta. But the RAF remained in control of the skies. On October 10, the Germans launched 120 sorties against the island. McElroy downed one of the attacking Messerschmitt 109s. The next day, the Luftwaffe sent up 216 sorties, and on October 12, the peak of their efforts, 279 sorties flew against Malta.

That day, a section of five Spitfires, including McElroy, took off and immediately encountered fourteen Messerschmitts. In the swirling dogfight, John got one of the attackers. As the Spits headed for home, McElroy spied a Junkers 88 and positioned himself in firing position astern of the enemy. Before he could fire, six more Messerschmitts bounced him. As they dove to attack, McElroy turned towards them and spent the next few minutes pulling gut-wrenching maneuvers, both to avoid the German guns and to get one of the enemy planes lined up for attack. He got his sights on one, bringing it down with a short burst, then turned to attack another. But the Germans had had enough, and they fled for home. John's entire flight lasted less than one hour, but when he landed, he found his aircraft riddled with machine gun bullet holes.

On October 15, he was airborne with six other pilots attacking a flight of 10 Junkers 88s escorted by 50 Messerschmitt 109s. He damaged one bomber so extensively that it was assessed as probably destroyed. But one of the enemy planes hit him, and he felt a fiery pain in one leg—a piece of shrapnel had wounded him. His cockpit filled with smoke. He tried desperately to bail out, but his canopy was jammed closed. The aircraft hurtled in a steep dive towards the sea. Fighting the controls, McElroy finally leveled out and made a crash landing back on Malta. The very next day, ignoring his leg wound, he went up again. Once more, he was shot up and had to crash land.

McElroy received the Distinguished Flying Cross and a promotion to flight lieutenant on October 19. The Luftwaffe accepted defeat in the Mediterranean, and the Germans and the Italian Regia Aeronautica flew only occasional reconnaissance sorties and strafing runs. On the 22nd, McElroy shared in destroying a Messerschmitt, and on the 27th, he damaged a Macchi MC 202.

In December, Flight Lieutenant John McElroy was posted back to England, beginning a tour as an instructor. On January 5, 1944, John arrived at No. 421 (Red Indian) Squadron. The McColl-Frontenac Oil Company, whose emblem was an "Indian head," had adopted the squadron. One of the company's products was Red Indian Aviation Motor Oil.

When John arrived, the squadron was flying Spitfire IXCs on defensive operations, offensive sweeps and escort duties. McElroy learned the fine art of dive-bombing and ground strafing. The pilots of No. 421 were active above the invasion forces on D-Day, but they saw none of the Luftwaffe.

On June 15, McElroy was leading a section of eight planes on an evening patrol when they flew straight into a formation of 20 Messerschmitt 109s and Focke-Wulf 190s. In the following wild fight, the squadron claimed seven enemy aircraft shot down, but one pilot and his Spitfire were lost. McElroy damaged one fighter, but another blasted away his port aileron and damaged the rest of his flight controls. He was at 15,000 feet, going 200 miles per hour, when his aircraft stalled. He put the plane into a steep glide. With skilled use of the tail elevators and rudder, McElroy reached an emergency airfield.

The next day, they left Tangmere and moved across the channel to Base 2 at Brazenville, France. Their orders emphasized bombing missions, armed reconnaissance and scrambles after intruding enemy. On June 23, Prime Minister Winston Churchill arrived to inspect and address 127 Wing. John flew one of the eight Spitfires that escorted the prime minister's aircraft back to England. By the end of the month, McElroy had shot two more German fighters out of the air.

By then he had finished his tour and was ordered back to the United Kingdom. Squadron Leader Jake Mitchner stepped up to take command of 421 Squadron.

On June 29, McElroy was promoted to squadron leader and took command of No. 416 (Lynx) Squadron. On July 27, while leading his pilots on

Air Marshall Breadner visits his newly appointed squadron leaders
in France. In the front row, third from the right is S/L J.F. McElroy.

a reconnaissance sortie near Alencon, John spotted two Focke-Wulf 190s preparing to land on a small grass strip. Circling and descending, he fired a broadside as one of the Focke-Wulfs touched down. The German plane rolled forward a short distance, then broke in two and ploughed into the hedge and trees at the end of the strip. McElroy's wingmen took out the second fighter.

When they weren't flying, the pilots and servicing crews spent their days sunbathing (when there was sun) and trying to catch up on their sleep. The Luftwaffe's nightly activities made it tough to get the approved eight hours of sleep at a stretch. Enemy activity encouraged them to deepen and improve their slit trenches.

The men played softball and cards, read books and took in the weekly movies in the mess provided by the Canadian Legion War Services. Occasionally, a keg of beer arrived by air from England. A few of the airmen did some local sightseeing, but in late July, several visits from Canadian Army Hospital nurses stirred up the most excitement.

August brought McElroy a bar to his Distinguished Flying Cross. It also brought the frenzied ground battle at the Falaise pocket in Normandy. Allied troops decimated the Nazi army, and the supporting fighter squadrons faced virtually no opposition as they destroyed thousands of fleeing enemy vehicles. As the Germans became more cautious about traveling in daylight, targets for the Spitfires became far fewer. The Spits were flying with 500-pound bombs slung under their wings, dropping them on road junctions, vehicle convoys, landing strips and bridges. Even motor launches in the Seine River and nearby canals were targets of accurate bombing and strafing by 416 Squadron pilots.

On September 4, 1944, John learned that he was the father of a baby girl. The squadron diarist wrote, "I guess that leave in Canada [when John got married]…wasn't in vain."

The squadron was with 127 Wing at Bazenville, Normandy, when McElroy took command the end of June. In August and September, the wing moved frequently to keep up with the ground forces—on August 28 to Iliers L'Evesque, Normandy; September 22 to Beauvechain (Le Culot) in Belgium; September 30 to Grave, Netherlands and October 23 to Melsbroek, Belgium.

On their last patrol from Le Culot, McElroy's section was over the Nijmegen Bridge. A bomb-carrying Focke-Wulf 190 and its escort, a Messerschmitt 109, flew into view, and McElroy attacked the 109. The German released his spare fuel tank and dove for the deck, streaming coolant behind him. Flight Lieutenant Dave Harling followed his leader in pursuit and gave the Messerschmitt a couple more bursts. The enemy pilot bailed out, and his aircraft crashed in flames. McElroy had scored his last victory in Europe. He had 13 ½ confirmed kills.

In Melsbroek, McElroy finished his tour. After flying 148 sorties, he was sent home to Canada. He and his family spent the last year of the war in Vancouver and Victoria, and he was released from the RCAF in September 1945. McElroy became a flight instructor in Vancouver and joined No. 442 (Auxiliary) Squadron. He was also employed as a rental car manager and a security officer, but he was itching to get back into a fighter cockpit.

His chance came in May 1948, when he was asked to recruit pilots to fly for Israel. The United Nations created the state of Israel on May 14, 1948. The next day, the Arab armies of Egypt, Syria, Jordan, Iraq, Saudi Arabia and Lebanon invaded the new Jewish state. Each country had its own designs on Palestine and had no intention of allowing the territory to be occupied and governed by the Jews. McElroy contacted several flyers and decided to volunteer himself. He and two friends, Jack Doyle and Denny Wilson, traveled by train to Toronto, then flew from London to Geneva and on to Rome. South African Airways took them to Haifa, Israel.

These Mahal (foreign volunteer) aviators became the unsung heroes of the Israeli War of Independence. Generally, these pilots' only motivation was to continue flying, and they had developed a taste for combat. But some, like Denny Wilson, had seen the horror of the Bergen-Belsen concentration camp. Others simply saw Israel as "the little guy" and went to its aid. Canadian soldiers, including infantrymen, tank drivers, artillerymen, technicians and specialists, also went to Israel's aid. Few were Jewish, but their story became one of brotherhood between Christians and Jews.

The Israeli Defence Forces had only one squadron of aircraft, No. 101 Fighter Squadron. Their ragtag assortment of airplanes included Messerschmitts, American P-51 Mustangs and Spitfires gathered from various Western nations, some by nefarious means—through illegal sales, the black market, and even (so rumour has it) theft. On December 18, John McElroy led a group of six Spitfires from Czechoslovakia through Yugoslavia to Israel. They chose the roundabout route to avoid curious air traffic controllers and stick to Israeli-friendly areas as much as possible.

Christmas in Israel should have been just another day, but in 1948, the 101 Squadron's Israeli airmen got together to produce a surprise Christmas dinner for the Mahal pilots. Denny Wilson reported that they had turkey with all the trimmings and then they were bussed to a church in Jaffa for Christmas services. The Canadians were touched by the experience.

The airmen were soon in action. On December 30, McElroy and Jack Doyle were flying a reconnaissance sortie near the Egyptian Air Force base of Bir Hana when they saw two Egyptian Macchi MC 205 Vs strafing an Israeli column. They cut in on the attackers, and Doyle quickly shot down the leader. The second aircraft peeled off and ran, but McElroy was on his tail. A short burst brought down the enemy plane. Both Egyptian aircraft were destroyed, and both pilots were killed.

By December 22, 1948, the Israelis appeared certain to rout the Egyptian army in the Sinai. Britain, under an agreement with Egypt, intervened and threatened Israel with retaliation should their forces enter the Suez Canal zone. The RAF kept a close eye on the war, sending reconnaissance missions from its Suez bases over the Sinai Peninsula. The British presence in the air above the desert increased.

On the morning of January 7, 1949, four Spitfire 18s from No. 208 RAF Squadron were flying a patrol from RAF Fayid to survey the land around Nitzana and Rafah. Their route took them to Abu Ageila, where they split up, two flying at 500 feet and the other two covering them at 1500 feet. The British flew east to the Negev-Sinai border, then north to Rafah. Meanwhile, McElroy and "Slick" Goodlin took off from the Israeli base at Qastina (Chatzor) in their old Spitfire 9s on a patrol of the front lines. It was the last day of the war; a cease-fire was due to come into effect that afternoon. Egyptian No. 2 Squadron Spitfires were also in the air. The Egyptians found an Israeli column near Rafah and attacked and destroyed three trucks.

Both the RAF Spitfires, flying low, and McElroy and Goodlin, at 16,000 to 18,000 feet, spotted the towering black smoke from the burning trucks at the same time. McElroy could see three columns of thick black smoke rising to about 1000 feet. He identified the convoy as Israeli, with a couple of light armoured vehicles, the trucks and some jeeps. At first, the Mahal could see no other aircraft. Then the four RAF Spitfires flew low over the vehicles. The Mahal pilots saw no broad red and white stripes on the tail rudders, so the airplanes were assumed to be enemy. Both McElroy and Goodlin thought they were strafing the convoy.

Israeli ground fire opened up and hit the British Spitfire flying in number two position following Flying Officer Geoff Cooper; Pilot Officer Frank Close bailed out of the burning aircraft. Amid the smoke, scattered cloud and blowing sand, the British probably never saw the Israeli planes. Close suffered a mild concussion and broken jaw when his head hit the tail of his aircraft. Cooper joined the other two fighters flown by Flying Officer Tim McElhaw and Pilot Officer Ron Sayers. Both Cooper and McElhaw had previously shot down Royal Egyptian Air Force Spitfires that had attacked the RAF base at Ramat David.

After watching Close's parachute descend, McElroy turned south, trying to see the other airplanes. Goodlin broke radio silence to warn McElroy: "There's an enemy aircraft at twelve o'clock, right in front of us!" The RAF airplanes were about 3000 feet below the Israelis, who dove to attack and started firing, peppering the RAF planes with bullets. Pieces flew off the wings of one plane, and the smoking aircraft plunged in a steep dive straight into the sand dunes. Ron Sayers could not get out in time.

Goodlin followed his target, Cooper, climbing through the sandy mist to about 16,000 feet. Cooper rolled and dove back toward Goodlin, guns blazing and exhaust smoke rolling out from under both wings. The slower Spit 9 had better maneuverability and was quickly in an ideal firing position. Cooper took strikes on his engine cowling, and he rolled over and bailed out. Then Goodlin saw the RAF roundel.

McElroy had spotted McElhaw orbiting Close's wreckage. Without the red and white tail markings, McElroy knew the other Spitfire was not one of their own. He got his sights on the unknown aircraft and let fly, striking it down the fuselage and the engine. McElroy's Spitfire suffered damage to its propeller and tail section from pieces of debris that flew off McElhaw's aircraft.

On the ground, Israeli forces captured McElhaw. Cooper evaded the troops, and some Bedouins helped him to a small Egyptian border post. Both Israeli aircraft returned to Chatzor and flew victory rolls before landing. Only then did McElroy learn that they had shot down RAF aircraft. At first McElroy did not believe it, because the British fighters were not supposed to be in that area.

Then confirmation came by telephone. Horrified, McElroy went pale, and his knees buckled. The next day, the 101 Squadron pilots sent a telegram to No. 208 Squadron: "Sorry about yesterday, but you were on the wrong side of the fence. Come over and have a drink sometime. You will see many familiar faces." McElroy visited McElhaw, then a POW in Tel Aviv, and reported a "perfectly civil conversation."

According to the 101 Squadron's historical records, John stayed in Israel until "at least March 1949," and then left the country. Uncertain of the consequences of shooting down RAF aircraft and fearful of the reception that might await him, he lingered in the United States. In April 1951, when it became clear that he would not be arrested for attacking British airplanes, and when the RCAF began building again for the Korean War, John McElroy re-enlisted. As a flying officer he served as an instructor, then joined No. 421 Squadron flying Sabres on NATO duty in Europe. He was promoted to flight lieutenant in January 1956.

McElroy retired from the air force in November 1964 and moved to London, Ontario, to pursue new challenges as a real estate salesman.

CHAPTER SIX

Gunners
Clarence Bentley Sutherland and Peter Engbrecht

ALTHOUGH FIGHTER PILOTS TYPICALLY EARNED THE TITLE "ACE," they were not the only aircrew members to down enemy machines. In Bomber Command, each aircraft required a pilot, navigator, flight engineer, bomb aimer, wireless operator and at least two gunners. Each trade was essential to the success of the bomber's mission. Without gunners, the aircraft was defenceless. Protection from marauding enemy fighters, vital to the continued life of the airplane, was vested in the vigilance, quick judgment and skilled marksmanship of the gunners, all performed in the blackest of night conditions. Only gunners had the means—guns—to keep an enemy aircraft away from their bomber. The problem with awarding ace status to a gunner is that he rarely shot down the enemy in isolation. Most victories were shared because the other gunners in the aircraft were usually firing at the same time, often at the same target.

Two Canadian gunners who were credited with shooting down more than the required five enemies for ace status were Sergeant Peter Engbrecht and Pilot Officer Clarence Bentley Sutherland.

Engbrecht flew as the mid-upper gunner in Halifax bombers with No. 424 (RCAF) Squadron of No. 6 Canadian Bomber Group. Sutherland was a tail gunner and then a mid-upper gunner in the Lancaster bombers of No. 207 (RAF) Squadron in No. 5 Bomber Group. Engbrecht is credited with 8½ kills, and Sutherland with at least 7 enemy aircraft destroyed and 1 damaged.

Clarence Sutherland was born on June 22, 1922, to James and Margaret Sutherland and raised on a farm near Truro, Nova Scotia. Peter Engbrecht was born in Poltavka, Russia, and raised in Winnipeg, but he called Summerside, PEI, his home when he enlisted.

Both men trained in Canada as air gunners under the British Commonwealth Air Training Plan. Engbrecht was in England serving as ground crew when Sutherland's accuracy with his guns won him his air gunner's wings at No. 9 Bombing and Gunnery School in Mont-Joli, Québec.

Clarence Bentley Sutherland (1922–)

Clarence Sutherland enlisted in Halifax on July 29, 1942, on his third try. He had been working in the gold mines of northern Ontario when he made his first attempt to enlist at a mobile recruiting centre in North Bay. Rebuffed there, he tried again in Toronto. Both recruiting officers turned Clarence down because he had monocular vision—a birth defect that had left him with only one functioning eye. In Halifax, he explained that his aptitude for

Pilot Officer Clarence B. Sutherland, DFC and Bar.

air gunnery was proven because he only needed one eye to pick sparrows off the barn roof with his rifle. The examining officer bought the story and decided to give Sutherland a chance.

On April 2, 1943, Clarence qualified as an air gunner and was promoted to sergeant. Later that month, Sutherland was sent to New York City to join 16,000 U.S. troops for the ocean voyage to Britain aboard HMT *Queen Elizabeth*. After his indoctrination at No. 3 Personnel Reception Centre in Bournemouth, Clarence reported to No. 1654 Heavy Conversion Unit, where airmen crewed up with the other bomber tradesmen. Choosing a crew was an exercise in self-preservation. You wanted mates who were good at their jobs and could perform well under the stress of wartime flying. Crews had 10 days to choose among themselves or be arbitrarily assigned. Sutherland ended up on a crew captained by Flight Lieutenant Doug Smith, a New Zealander flying with the RAF.

On October 2, 1943, Sutherland was promoted to flight sergeant. After training on four-engine bombers, the crew was sent as a group to No. 207 (RAF) Squadron at Spilesby, Lincolnshire, flying Lancasters. They arrived on November 23, 1943, and the crew flew their first nine sorties against Berlin.

Sutherland flew his first 21 sorties as a tail gunner. His turret was a Fraser-Nash 20, equipped with four .303 machine guns. Clarence's first taste of night operations came on December 16, 1943, when he flew as a spare gunner on a raid to Berlin. His second trip was the first with his crew, to Berlin on December 23. On the flight, Sutherland downed his first German night fighter. The enemy pilot had just shot down a neighbouring Lancaster, which dove away in flames. As the aircrew watched, the

Junkers 88 lined up on them. But Sutherland was quicker, and his shots brought the enemy down with one wing blazing. It was the first German night fighter ever shot down over Berlin.

The remaining 14 sorties of Sutherland's operational tour were spent in the mid-upper turret, commanding two Browning .303 machine guns in the Fraser-Nash 50 turret. His good friend, Flying Officer Wallace McIntosh, occupied the rear turret. The top turret had a great all-around view of the sky, but it was tough to get in and out of in a heated flying suit, Mae West life vest and parachute harness. Of all the bombers, the Lancaster was the most difficult for a gunner to bail from, and the ride was anything but comfortable. Pilots rarely flew straight and level until the final bombing. En route, they wove and bobbed, turned and banked. This made the bomber a more difficult target for night fighters and gave the gunners a chance to look under their aircraft for enemy planes coming up from below.

Clarence almost did not survive one trip to Berlin. On January 30, it was so cold that icicles began to form on his oxygen mask. In the uninsulated turret, with the wind whistling through gaping cracks, his mask froze solid. When he did not respond to calls on the intercom, the pilot sent the wireless operator back with a spare oxygen bottle. The operator revived Clarence, and they descended to 10,000 feet. On the return trip, Sutherland's head was pounding, and he could

P/O C.B. Sutherland, DFC and Bar, and F/O W. McIntosh, DFC and Bar, DFM, gunners on the same crew, who were the top scoring gunner aces of the RCAF and RAF respectively.

hardly keep his eyes open, a dangerous problem for a gunner.

After flying with eight different pilots, Clarence ended up on a crew skippered by Wing Commander J.F. Grey. He considered this a piece of luck, since

Grey was an experienced bomber pilot and was slated to take command of No. 207 Squadron. Sutherland was commissioned as a pilot officer on May 2, 1944.

On D-Day, June 6, 1944, No. 207 Squadron's Lancasters attacked Caen, supporting the Canadian division that had landed on the Normandy beaches. On the night of June 7–8, No. 5 Group sent 112 Lancasters and 10 Mosquitos to the Forêt de Cerisy to attack the important six-way road junction halfway between Bayeux and Saint-Lô. Planners believed the surrounding woods were harbouring fuel dumps and German tanks preparing to counter-attack the Allied landing forces. During the raid, Sutherland and McIntosh, flying in Lancaster *M*, won the Distinguished Flying Cross. McIntosh had previously won the Distinguished Flying Medal.

Just after the crew crossed the enemy coast at 8000 feet, McIntosh sighted a Junkers 88 silhouetted against the moon, closing to attack on the left side. He warned Grey, who took the necessary combat maneuvers as McIntosh and Sutherland both opened fire. They hit the enemy aircraft with carefully placed bursts, and it spun towards the ground with both engines on fire. The German plane was still flaming when it disappeared into a cloud. Almost immediately, the wireless operator warned the crew of another Junkers 88 coming into range, and both gunners poured devastating bursts of fire into the oncoming attacker. At 150 yards, it exploded under the Lancaster's tail. Twenty minutes later, the gunners engaged a third enemy, a Messerschmitt 410. Their accurate fire forced the enemy to fall away, and his aircraft caught fire before it hit the sea. The gunners claimed two Junkers 88s and the Messerschmitt 410 as destroyed. Bomber Command boss Air Marshall Harris telephoned the base commander demanding to know, "Who the hell were those guys?"

The base's commanding officer and Air Vice Marshall Ralph Cochrane, Air Officer Commanding No. 5 Group, recommended both gunners for immediate awards of the Distinguished Flying Cross. Their citation noted: "Flying Officer McIntosh and Pilot Officer Sutherland defended their aircraft with great skill and resolution and undoubtedly played a large part in its safe return. Their achievement was worthy of high praise." Sutherland was further cited for his "courage, calmness and skill."

On the night of July 12–13, No. 5 Group sent Lancasters to attack French railway targets. The squadron's targets were Culmont and Tours. The crew was again flying aircraft *M*. They were at 4000 feet on a black night at 0157 hours when the rear gunner sighted a Messerschmitt 109 just above them in the starboard rear quarter. McIntosh watched the enemy bank and then start on a curve of pursuit. Both the Lancaster gunners fired, hitting the enemy's nose and starboard wing. They continued shooting until the aircraft burst into flames, dove sharply and exploded when it hit the ground. The gunners claimed the Messerschmitt 109 as destroyed.

The last of a series of raids on Stuttgart was planned for the night of July 28–29. The skies were wild over the target as German fighters intercepted the stream of 494 Lancasters under a bright moon and shot down 39 of the bombers. Lancaster *M* was attacked five times. The gunners destroyed two fighters and drove off the rest. The crew was at 15,000 feet when a Focke-Wulf 190 attacked. Both gunners poured withering fire at the enemy plane, hitting its engine and wings. The German aircraft caught fire, parts falling to the earth, and it spiraled downwards in flames. Crewmembers saw a glow in the cloud immediately after the enemy aircraft entered it and claimed the 190 as destroyed.

Twenty-two minutes later, flying at 11,000 feet, a Junkers 88 dove in on them. The gunners hit it on the wings, the nose and the starboard engine. The German aircraft continued its dive into the ground, where it exploded and was claimed as destroyed.

The raid won Sutherland a bar to his Distinguished Flying Cross. Clarence's recommendation read:

"Pilot Officer Sutherland is an air gunner with a fine operational record. He has participated in the destruction of seven enemy aircraft and damaged one. Three have been destroyed since the award of the Distinguished Flying Cross. His aircraft have been in combat on other occasions, and his accurate gunnery and coolness under fire have been outstanding."

Sutherland's last flight with Grey was on August 5, 1944. The target was the St-Leu-d'Esserent V-1 bomb storage site. Bombing conditions were good for Sutherland's 36th sortie, which marked the completion of his tour of operations. En route to the area, a night fighter jumped their aircraft, and the enemy's accurate fire put out two of their engines. They were likely to lose another engine, so Grey ordered all equipment jettisoned to lighten the load. He eventually nursed his damaged Lancaster to an emergency aerodrome at Manston. The aircraft landed after 3 hours and 50 minutes flying with only two engines and an unusable hydraulic system.

Pilot Officer C. B. Sutherland was awarded his operational wings and posted away on August 18 to training duties. He was repatriated to Canada on October 22 and promoted to flying officer on November 2, 1944. When Clarence took his release from the RCAF on February 9, 1945, he was the top air gunner in Bomber Command.

Sutherland learned that the air force was photographing and mapping Canada's north. He had been interested in the North and in photography for some time, so he wanted to be a part of this project. For postwar service, he had to resign his commission, and so he rejoined as a leading aircraftsman on June 27, 1946. He went to learn the photography trade at No. 1 Photo Establishment in Ottawa. After months of air force bureaucrats procrastinating and no progress in his trades training, Clarence again took his release on December 16, 1946.

In 1947 Clarence married Margaret. They raised a son, James, and a daughter, Marion. After leaving the RCAF, Clarence trained as a chef with the Murray's restaurant chain in Toronto and then began a career in construction, eventually becoming the mason foreman on the first Toronto subway. Wages were much better in the U.S. than in Canada, so in 1955, he moved to Chicago and stayed until he retired in 1992 and moved to Florida.

Peter Engbrecht (1923–1991)

The Engbrechts came to Canada from Russia in 1923, when Peter was three years old. The Mennonite family settled in Winnipeg, Manitoba, where Peter finished high school and then went to trade school to learn to be a blacksmith. When he joined the air force on November 17, 1941, in Winnipeg, he gave his address as Water Street, Summerside, PEI. Peter was one of an estimated 4500 Canadian Mennonites who joined active military service despite their church's pacifist beliefs.

Peter Engbrecht spent the first two years of his air force service as ground crew, trained as a maintenance assistant. He was posted overseas in 1942, but he repeatedly tried to remuster to aircrew. Peter wanted to be a pilot. Finally, in the summer of 1943, he began air gunnery training and received the highest gunnery score in the school's history He soon put that skill to good use.

Sergeant Peter Engbrecht admires the two swastikas painted on his upper turret to mark his first dual success against Nazi night fighters.

After he completed gunnery school, learning the trade using Vickers machine guns at the rear doors of Fairey Battle aircraft, Peter was promoted to sergeant and had an air gunner's wing sewn on the left breast of his uniform tunic. He went to the Personnel Reception Centre at Bournemouth and then on to No. 23 Operational Training Unit at RAF Station Pershope to train for a night-bomber crew, flying in the Halifax heavy bomber. At Pershope, Peter became part of the bomber crew he would fly with on the requisite number of sorties to complete a tour of operations. The whole crew moved on to No. 1659 Heavy Conversion Unit in Topcliffe to train on the Halifax bomber they would fly against the enemy.

In July 1943, No. 6 (RCAF) Group was formed as a totally Canadian air group composed of eight Canadian squadrons, including No. 424 (Tiger) Squadron. They were based in Skipton-on-Swale and were equipped with the Handley-Page Halifax III. The squadron's primary targets were in occupied Europe. They flew bombing raids on industrial complexes, communications centres, port facilities and the V-1 rocket sites being built along the coast.

Flying Officer O.J.G. "Jimmy" Keys, an American flying in the RCAF, skippered Engbrecht's crew. They reported to No. 424 (RCAF) Squadron on May 12, 1944. Peter was assigned the top turret position, a Boulton Paul mid-upper turret armed with two .303 machine guns. The mid-upper gunner had a nice view, but the position was cold and cramped. Sergeant G.C. Gillanders claimed the rear turret.

Peter's trial by fire came the night of May 27, 1944, during an attack on the Bourg-Léopold, Belgium military camp and supply lines. Night fighters attacked the lumbering aircraft, Halifax *HX 316 D*, no less than 14 times. The first enemy fighter knocked out the rear guns, leaving Peter alone and armed with only one serviceable machine gun to defend his airplane and crew.

He hit the 109, which blew up in his sights. Peter successfully warded off the remaining 13 attacks, and his guns brought down two of the attackers, a Focke-Wulf 190 and a Messerschmitt 110, with skill and accuracy. Not that Peter was keeping track—he was far too busy swinging his guns in complete circles to get his sights on the enemies swarming like bees around the damaged Halifax.

At the first flash of the attack, his mouth went instantly arid with fear. His mouth was still dry when the attackers disappeared, but the fear was long gone. Silently, he congratulated himself for the extra time he took before takeoff to polish the Perspex of his turret. Thanks to his efforts, it had stayed clear and did not impair his vision. He cursed under his breath as he slipped and stumbled on the brass cartridges littering the floor of the air-craft—he was going through belts of ammunition in record time. He could smell the cordite even through the rubber oxygen mask strapped to his face. Suddenly it was all over. When his guns stopped chattering, relative silence returned, except for the roar of the four Bristol Hercules engines and the rattle of metal from the vibrating fuselage. Peter's night vision slowly recovered from the glare of his guns' muzzle flashes. Still, the tension did not lessen. The entire crew remained nerve-edge alert until they entered the circuit of their home aerodrome.

On the eve of D-Day, the squadron flew bombing raids against the enemy gun batteries at Houlgatte, followed by attacks on German defences, freight yards and rocket sites.

On June 10, two weeks after the initial success of May 27, they took off, again in Halifax *D*, to bomb a railway junction at Étampes, south of Paris near Versailles. The Pathfinders' marking was accurate but late, and the bombing spread from the railway marshalling yards into the town. Between 400 and 500 houses were destroyed, and 133 people were killed. On the way home at 4000 feet, a flare popped to life on their starboard side. They could see a Messerschmitt 110 silhouetted in the light. Gillanders and Engbrecht opened fire. The enemy aircraft appeared to lose control and dove straight down, exploding on the ground seconds later. Within a minute, Peter spotted a Messerschmitt 109 closing in to attack. Both the gunners again let loose. A small glow started at the nose of the enemy fighter, rapidly growing into flames. As it went down, it flew into clouds, and a few seconds later the whole cloud lit up. The crew claimed two enemy aircraft destroyed.

On the night of July 4–5, their target was a V-1 store in a large cave at St-Leu-d'Esserent, north of Paris. They followed a daylight raid on the same target by Bomber Command's 617 Squadron. Cloud littered the sky, but the attacks were mostly success-ful. A group of 231 Lancasters and 15 Mosquitos dropped 1000-pound bombs, cutting all German access to the store. The drop was accurate, but

German fighters engaged the force, and 13 Lancasters were lost.

The crew was flying Halifax *F* at 12,600 feet when a Messerschmitt 109 bounced the bomber at 0040 hours. The enemy fired, and the two gunners replied. Their tracer bounced off the fighter, and the Messerschmitt broke away. Other crewmembers watched the fighter go down in flames, and an explosion lit up the clouds. About an hour later, a Focke-Wulf 190 tried its luck with the bomber, which had descended to 5000 feet for the trip home. The Halifax crew saw the enemy aircraft at 200 yards on their starboard side. Both gunners opened fire and continued to lace the fighter with bullets until, at 100 yards, it caught fire, dove out of control straight down and exploded against the earth. The two gunners had destroyed two more aircraft.

Peter Engbrecht officially became an ace on his next sortie to Brunswick, when he shared in the destruction of two more enemy fighters, bringing his total to six. Throughout August, the crew flew sorties to drop bombs ahead of the Allied soldiers advancing towards Germany. They also dropped mines in the approaches of European ports as far away as Norway.

On August 4, 1944, the *London Gazette* announced that Sergeant Peter Engbrecht of 424 (RCAF) Squadron had been awarded the Conspicuous Gallantry Medal (Flying). The award recognized

Flying Officer Peter Engbrecht, CGM.

his bravery in air operations against the enemy.
Since its inception in 1943 only 101 Conspicuous
Gallantry Medals (Flying) have been awarded, 12
to Canadians. Peter's citation read:

> *"As mid-upper gunner, this airman has partici-
> pated in several sorties and has proved himself to*

be an exceptionally cool and confident member of aircraft crew. On one occasion during a sortie his aircraft was subjected to 14 separate attacks by fighters. In the ensuing fights, Sergeant Engbrecht defended his aircraft with great skill and two of the attackers fell to his guns. In June 1944, he took part in an attack on a target in Northern France. On the return flight, his aircraft was attacked on two occasions by fighters. Sergeant Engbrecht engaged the enemy aircraft with deadly effect each time, and his brilliant shooting caused their destruction. His feats have been worthy of the greatest praise."

King George VI presented Engbrecht, now promoted to flight sergeant, with the medal at the Leeming RAF base on August 11, 1944.

The night of August 12–13, 137 Halifaxes and 242 Lancasters launched an experimental raid on Brunswick to determine how accurately each crew could bomb based only on target information provided by the onboard H2S radar equipment. The test failed; there was no concentration of the bombing, and some crews mistook towns 20 miles away for Brunswick.

That same night 36 Halifaxes, including *MZ 802 G* carrying Peter Engbrecht and Gordon Gillanders, carried out a raid on a German troop concentration and a road junction near Falaise where Canadian troops were pushing back the Wehrmacht on the ground. The bombing was effective, and no Allied aircraft were lost. Reports from the Canadian soldiers complimented the tenacity of the aircrews in continuing their attacks in spite of the heavy flak barrage. The ground troops sent a message that they were glad to be on the same side as Bomber Command. All squadron members were thankful that they had not flown on the nights that Allied aircraft had mistakenly dropped bombs on the Canadian troops in Falaise.

During a furious night of combat, Engbrecht added two more victories, a Messerschmitt 109 and a Messerschmitt 110, bringing his official score to eight destroyed aircraft and one shared, a total of 8½. He had watched as the 110's pilot shot down a nearby Halifax before turning its attention to Peter's bomber. Engbrecht and Gillanders poured converging streams of fire into the attacking plane. The Messerschmitt burst into flames and exploded. Peter's crew landed in an unscathed Halifax. It was his last kill, but four nights later, homeward bound from a raid on Kiel, Peter and his fellow gunner drove off an unidentified enemy aircraft that was last seen burning as it fled.

Christmas 1944 was especially bountiful for the members of 424 Squadron. They had been adopted by the city of Hamilton, and its Tiger Squadron Committee sent each member a Christmas parcel. The packages contained goodies such as razor blades, needles, thread, toilet paper, hot chocolate, peanuts, Oxo, cheese, crackers and—a squadron favourite—canned chicken. Another gift was thousands of cigarettes from various donors.

Not long before his time in Europe ended, Peter received his commission. Pilot Officer Peter Engbrecht finished his tour of operations. He returned to Canada and left the service.

Peter Engbrecht did not stay out of uniform long. He rejoined the RCAF with a short service commission as a flying officer. At the end of his five-year contract, he was let go because he did not have sufficient formal education to be an officer. Relinquishing his wartime commission, Peter returned in the rank of leading aircraftsman and was trained as an air defence technician. He spent much of his time at Canadian Forces Base Beausejour, Manitoba, a long-range radar site that was part of the NORAD air defence system. In 1971, he was recognized and honoured as an outstanding airman for his service defending the continent against air attack.

Just before he retired from the Canadian Forces, with a total of 28½ years of service, Master Corporal Peter Engbrecht was selected as the 1975 RCAF Association's first Airman of the Year, an award created to recognize his outstanding service. He was flown to Ottawa, and on September 29, he stood on the dais before the Parliament Buildings and took the salute of 200 delegates on parade— a rare honour for an enlisted man. At the banquet that night, His Excellency Roland Mitchener, the governor general, saluted one of the only non-pilot aces of World War II.

In December 1975, Peter retired to his home in Whitewater, Manitoba. At age 68, on April 23, 1991, Peter Engbrecht died at home.

CHAPTER SEVEN

Donald John "Don" Sheppard
Blue Pacific Skies
(1924–)

CANADIANS SELDOM KNOW MUCH OF THE HISTORY OF WORLD War II beyond the European theatre. But the war was truly a global conflict, and few nations did not feel its effects. With the focus on the United States' role in the Pacific Ocean after the Japanese attack on Pearl Harbor on December 7, 1941, there is still little attention paid to Canadians' involvement in that area. Yet more than 7500 Canadian aviators served in the Pacific and in the China, Burma and India theatres even before the Japanese invasion. Not much is known of the RCAF fighter pilots who flew Hurricanes, Spitfires and Beaufighters in southeast Asia, and even less information is included in our history books about the Canadians who flew Hellcats and Corsairs from British Royal Navy aircraft carriers. The environment where they flew and fought was even more hostile than the European theatre.

In 1942, all three sons of Ross Sheppard, a Toronto lawyer, and his wife, Mabel Heron, a school-teacher, were in the Royal Navy. The eldest, William, had joined as a university student in 1940

Lieutenant D. J. Sheppard, RCNVR, DSC

and was studying in Brighton, England, to become an officer. Robert and Don were drawn to naval aviation. Robert, one year older than Donald, was an officer in a Toronto corps of sea cadets, while Don's military exposure consisted of training in the 48th Highlanders militia regiment while he was a student at Lawrence Park Collegiate.

The younger brothers enlisted as pilot candidates; 18-year-old Don "borrowed" the application from Robert's desk. He mailed it to the British navy and was invited to the Royal Navy Air Station at Lee-on-Solent on the south coast of England to be interviewed for aircrew training. He was found acceptable to the Fleet Air Arm, but at first he was offered training as an observer. Don wanted to fly planes, and he negotiated. If the Royal Navy did not want him as a pilot, he argued, the Royal Canadian Air Force did. He won the argument and was sent a few miles away to Gosport, just across the harbour from the city of Portsmouth, to take basic training on Pilot Course No. 38. Robert soon followed on Course No. 51.

Training at HMS *St. Vincent* (a training establishment) emphasized nautical skills. Don learned to sail and tie knots and took classes in ship recognition. The sailors also stood night guard duty, ever vigilant for air raids. Don received his elementary flight training courtesy of the United States Navy. His first posting was to USN Air Station Grosse Ile, Michigan, near Detroit and not far from his home in Toronto. He passed the pilot training course and went on to flight training at USN Air Station Pensacola, Florida, which was the only land-based facility capable of teaching pilots how to land on an aircraft carrier. On May 5, 1943, Don Sheppard became a midshipman in the Royal Navy Volunteer Reserve and had his navy wings pinned to his lower left sleeve, above the gold rank braid.

Sheppard won his wings flying the Chance-Vought F4U Corsair. While the Spitfire became the most famous fighter of the war, the Royal Navy found its version, the Seafire, somewhat fragile for operations aboard an aircraft carrier, and supply was limited. Therefore, the navy was thrilled when the United States Navy offered half its inventory of Corsairs to the British under the Lend-Lease Agreement. The other half went to the United States Marine Corps. The high-performance Corsair had a 2000 horse-power engine and a top speed of 400 miles per hour.

After receiving his wings, Sheppard went to USNAS Miami, Florida, for the Royal Navy Fighter Course, then to USNAS Lewiston, Maine, to convert to the Martlet V (the British name for the Grumman F4F Wildcat). Sheppard was promoted to acting sub-lieutenant (air) on October 22, 1943 and sent to USNAS Brunswick, Maine, to join No. 1835 Royal Navy Squadron. The squadron was flying Corsair IIs, but it disbanded in November. Sheppard was sent to join No. 1836 Squadron. In January 1944, the squadron formed the 47th Naval Fighter Wing with No. 1834 Squadron. With 14 Corsairs, the aircrews embarked aboard the carrier *Victorious*.

HMS *Victorious* was a fairly new ship. She was launched in September 1939 and commissioned on May 15, 1941. The carrier was superbly armoured and able to shake off the kamikaze attacks she suffered in 1945, unlike many of the U.S. carriers that had wooden flight decks. HMS *Victorious* was a veteran of the battle with the *Bismarck* just nine days after her commissioning and had made a strike on the *Tirpitz* in 1942. She was refitted at the U.S. navy yard in Norfolk during the winter of 1942–43 and then loaned to the U.S. navy for service in the Pacific Fleet. During her time in U.S. service, she was called the USS *Robin*. She was returned to the British and came home to Scapa Flow in the Orkney Islands near the end of 1943, and in March 1944, HMS *Victorious* participated in the battle with the *Tirpitz*.

King George VI witnessed one of Don Sheppard's initial flights from HMS *Victorious*. The King had been invited aboard to watch carrier operations. Don was flying with a failed air speed indicator. As he tried to land, he slammed his airplane onto the deck at high speed. When his tail hook caught the arresting wire, the aircraft jerked to a halt and tipped forward, but not enough, thankfully, to damage the propeller. Later, the King praised the pilots for their keenness and professionalism, but all the aviators wanted to hear was an announcement of an increased risk allowance—it was not forthcoming.

Late in March 1944, HMS *Victorious*, with her squadron of Corsair pilots including twenty-year-old pilot Don Sheppard, sailed into the North Sea. The vessel's destination and mission was unknown to the airmen until the admiral assembled them in the officers' wardroom. He told them that they were sailing to provide cover for the Fairey Barracuda dive-bombers that were aiming for the *Tirpitz*. Although they would be flying at 18,000 feet,

Corsairs on the flight deck of HMS *Victorious* in preparation for an air strike against the Japanese in 1945.

the pilots were nervous that their first combat with their Corsairs would be against Germany's greatest and most dangerous warship. The Allies found the German battleship on April 2 anchored in Norway's Kaa Fjord, and the attacks put *Tirpitz* out of action for three months.

HMS *Victorious* became the first Royal Navy aircraft carrier to operationally use the F4U Corsair fighter. Until May, HMS *Victorious* and her air arm attacked enemy shipping off the coast of Norway while the British ship returned to Scapa Flow.

In 1944, Sub-Lieutenant Don Sheppard, RNVR, discovered that he could transfer to the Royal Canadian Navy Volunteer Reserve with no loss of rank and stay with 1836 squadron. He promptly followed his Canadian loyalty and transferred. His choice felt all the more sweet since he was the lone Canadian aviator on the ship.

In June 1944, HMS *Victorious* and her air squadron sailed to join the Eastern Fleet and arrived in the Indian Ocean in July. The fleet had six new aircraft carriers, two battleships and six cruisers. Twelve destroyers escorted the flotilla. It was a formidable force. Their first operational attack was against the oil storage facilities and the airfields of Sabang, Sumatra (now a part of Indonesia).

In August, Lieutenant Colonel R.C. "Ronnie" Hay of the Royal Marines took command of the wing. He chose one pilot from each of the three squadrons to fly with him, including Don Sheppard as his number two. On January 4, 1945, the section was flying high cover for an attack on the Japanese installations at Pangkalan Brandan. Sheppard spotted an enemy Oscar (slang for the Nakajima Ki-43 Hyabusa) trying to sneak between his group and the flights lower down. The Canadian pilot dove to the attack, but before he could shoot, the Japanese pilot rolled his aircraft and bailed out. Unfortunately, the enemy pilot fell from his parachute harness to his death. Don climbed back up to rejoin his mates. He then saw another Oscar below and again maneuvered for an attack. At about 200 yards he opened up with his four wing-mounted .50 calibre machine guns. The enemy aircraft blew up. Sheppard had his first two kills.

The wing continued attacks on Japanese oil installations and airfields. Ronnie Hay was supposed to be the air coordinator, but he did more air fighting than coordinating. Don recalled Hay telling him the first time they flew together, "Now, Sheppard, your job is to make sure nothing happens to me. I am the most important guy up there, and I don't care what happens to you, but you are to make sure nothing happens to me. Never take your eyes off me."

Don reminisced about a flight later in January:

"I stuck to him like glue. Every time we ran into fighters he would take them on instead of sticking to his job of air coordinator—he would rush right in. We came in high over the target (that had been bombed), and Hay had a camera in his aircraft, and we stayed behind to take pictures. Of course, the Japanese pilots would come up after us, and here we were the only four Fleet Air Arm pilots left over the target! It was a great opportunity to shoot aircraft down, but very dangerous."

Sheppard shot down one Japanese Tojo fighter on the first attack against Palembang on January 24th, 1945, and Major Hay got two. Five days later, during the second attack, Hay and Sheppard shared two more victories (a Tojo and an Oscar).

Don Sheppard received the Distinguished Service Cross for gallantry and meritorious services before the enemy. The Distinguished Service Cross is the only purely naval decoration, awarded to officers of the rank of commander and below, warrant officers of His Majesty's Fleet and RAF officers flying with the Fleet Air Arm.

Don's brother Robert was also flying Corsairs aboard HMS *Formidable* in the British Pacific Fleet. On March 21, 1945, during takeoff for a training flight, Robert's left wheel struck a ramp projection on the forward flight deck. Trying to gain control, he climbed steeply, stalled and crashed into the sea. He did not survive. On hearing the news, Don flew over to HMS *Formidable* to learn more but there was little the sailors could tell him about what had happened. The aircraft had gone into the sea, and nothing was recovered. The fleet continued underway to support the United States Navy in the battle for Okinawa.

On May 4, Sheppard was airborne on combat air patrol in the Okinawa area when radar detected a Japanese fighter circling at 20,000 feet above the fleet. The Japanese pilot was obviously reporting on the ships for the kamikaze fliers. Sheppard left his section behind, dropped his external fuel tank and gave chase. The enemy aircraft, a Judy (slang for a Yokosuka D4Y3 Suisei bomber), was no match for the powerful Corsair. Soon Don had the Japanese plane in his sights and blasted away with his wing-mounted guns. The Judy exploded in a ball of fire, engulfing the speeding Corsair, and the explosive wake and burning debris set Don's fabric-covered elevators on fire. Don's whole section was forced to return to the ship. The entire fleet had to follow the aircraft carrier and turn into wind so the planes could land. The ships' captains were none too pleased, as running into wind made them more vulnerable to attack. When Don landed, he found his rudder and tailplane were wrinkled from the heat. He had earned his fifth confirmed victory (the two shared only counted for ½ each), becoming the only Canadian Corsair ace and the first pilot in the Fleet Air Arm to achieve ace status.

Don was well aware of the damage a kamikaze could do. He was on the bridge of *Victorious* on May 9, 1945, when one of the suicide pilots aimed directly for the ship. The carrier's guns stopped the Japanese attack, but the plane exploded about 50 feet from Sheppard. He could hardly believe that he wasn't hit, and the carrier suffered no damage.

With two years of combat flying under his belt, Don was sent home to Canada on leave. No one knew he was coming, so when he knocked on the door his "mother's jaw nearly hit the floor." He was supposed to be home for a couple of months before returning for the final assault on Japan. Don was at the family cottage on Lake Simcoe when he learned that the United States had dropped two atomic bombs on Hiroshima and Nagasaki. Japan's capitulation followed quickly.

Don's wartime service as a navy fighter pilot was over, but his military career was just beginning. He decided to remain in the Royal Canadian Navy, transferring from the RCNVR on June 1, 1946. He had been promoted to lieutenant, with seniority backdated to February 9, 1945. Sheppard served in the newly formed air squadrons of the navy and in various staff positions at Naval Headquarters. In 1952, he was named Naval Assistant to the Commandant of the Canadian Joint Air Training School in Rivers, Manitoba. With the encouragement of his army colleagues, he made another first for a navy pilot and qualified for his paratrooper's wings. He also earned his watchkeeping ticket as a surface ship's deck officer in 1948. On July 1, 1958, he was given command of the Canadian navy's destroyer escort, HMCS *Fraser II*, stationed on the West Coast. He was promoted to lieutenant commander in 1953 and commander in 1958.

Along the way, Don Sheppard convinced Gwendolyn Alice Falls to become his wife. They have five children, sons Robert and Michael and daughters Christine, Nancy and Susan. After a distinguished peacetime career, Don Sheppard was piped ashore on January 1, 1974. He had an impressive 2655 flying hours accumulated on 26 aircraft and had made 112 carrier landings. After short stays in Halifax and British Columbia, the Sheppards bought a farm just outside Belleville, Ontario, where they raised beef and bees until 1984 when they moved to Aurora, a convenient location halfway between Toronto and the family cottage on Lake Simcoe. Now in his 80s, Commander Don Sheppard spends pleasant hours walking his dog.

CHAPTER EIGHT

Hugh Charles "Charlie" Trainor
From Spud Island to Stalag Luft I
(1916–2004)

CHARLIE TRAINOR BEGAN FLYING SPITFIRE VB FIGHTERS operationally with No. 411 Squadron on May 11, 1943. All year, the squadron flew bomber escorts and routine patrols, hardly ever seeing enemy aircraft. When they did encounter Luftwaffe fighters, the German pilots rarely deigned to engage.

Then, the last three days of June 1944, Flight Lieutenant Hugh Trainor made the grade as a marksman. He destroyed four enemy airplanes in those three days. And during the first four days of July he scored another 3½ times. The news on squadron for July 2 and 3 was that Flight Lieutenant Trainor did not "bag a Hun."

Hugh Charles Trainor was born in Charlottetown, PEI, on July 17, 1916, the son of a railway conductor. He completed high school in the island capital and then attended St. Dunstan's University (now the University of Prince Edward Island). After five years of study, Charlie graduated with a Bachelor of Arts degree. He led his class in academics each year. Charlie spent a year articling with a local

Squadron Leader Hugh C. Trainor, DSO, DFC and Bar.

lawyer, but the outbreak of war relieved him of the tedious study of statutes.

There was no recruiting centre on the Island, so Charlie took the ferry to the mainland and travelled to Moncton, New Brunswick, to enlist in the Royal Canadian Air Force. Because he had a university degree, he was sworn in with a commission as a pilot officer on February 16, 1940. From February 21 to April 28, he was attached to Eastern Air Command while he took lessons at the civilian flying club in Sydney, Nova Scotia. He was then posted to Toronto to attend No.1 Initial Training School, where he was introduced to air force life and the air force way of flying. The tall, slim young man was a sensation with Charlottetown girls when he went home on leave dressed in his air force blues.

Charlie was as keen at flight school as he had been at university. He was promoted to flying officer on October 5, 1940, and sent to No. 1 Service Flight Training School at Camp Borden, Ontario, where he learned to fly Yales, Harvards and Fleet Finches. He successfully completed basic flight training, and on July 20, 1941, proudly stood on his wings parade to have RCAF pilot's wings pinned to the left breast of his tunic. Because of his skill in the cockpit, Charlie stayed in Canada as a flying instructor. He was a conscientious, hard-working trainer and made his students feel quite at ease in the unfamiliar environment of the skies. Charlie taught at RCAF Station Trenton, at No. 9 Service Flight Training School in Summerside and No. 8 Service Flight Training School in Moncton. At Summerside, Charlie received another promotion, to flight lieutenant. After two years of badgering his superior officers with requests to be sent overseas, Charlie got his wish, and he sailed from Halifax on October 27, 1942.

After 10 days on the rolling North Atlantic, he arrived in Britain. Charlie was sent to No. 17 Advanced Flying Unit, where he was introduced to the intricacies of wartime flying. With the average rate of survival for aircrews being only eight sorties, the instructors at the AFU were trying hard to increase the students' chance of survival by making them more warlike aviators.

On January 5, 1943, Trainor was posted to No. 57 Operational Training Unit, where he began his love affair with the most famous fighter aircraft of World War II—the Supermarine Spitfire. This sleek, fast airplane epitomized the adventure of flying and the challenge of aerial combat. It was a single seat machine, which meant that instructors familiarized fledgling pilots with the controls and the cockpit layout and then sent them flying solo.

Hugh Trainor's first operational fighter squadron was No. 402 (City of Winnipeg) Squadron, where he stayed only a month before going to No. 411 (Grizzly Bear) Squadron. He reported for flying duty on May 11, 1943. The squadron, based at Redhill, Surrey, was flying Spitfire VBs almost daily on bomber escorts over the Continent, but pilots rarely encountered any German fighters. Also flying from Redhill was No. 401 Squadron, another Canadian squadron, part of No. 11 Fighter Group.

On May 17, Charlie's ground crewman helped strap him into the cockpit of Spitfire *BL 780*. He was in high spirits and full of adrenaline as he prepared for takeoff on his first operational sortie. At 0955, his left hand advanced the throttle, and his machine hurtled down the runway. As he gathered speed, the tail lifted, and almost before he knew it, he was airborne. The familiar feeling of flying, after training so long for his operational duty, was less than routine on this day. The squadron was tasked with escorting six USAAF Mitchell bombers to attack the airfield at Caen. Although 22 enemy Messerschmitt 109s were in the area, Charlie's squadron had no engagement with any of them.

Two days later, Trainor was flying aircraft *EP 173* in White Section on a convoy patrol over the English Channel. The days dragged on as the men flew routine patrols and bomber escorts but made no contact with the enemy. Charlie's trips were uneventful, except on July 6, when he was forced to return to base early because his hood had blown away on takeoff. On August 6, the three squadrons (401, 411 and 412) that made up No. 126 Airfield moved to a new base at Staplehurst, Kent.

On September 28, Flight Lieutenant Trainor returned to instructional duties with a posting at No. 41 Operational Training Unit. His skill as a teacher was still valued. In mid-October, the squadrons moved again, to Biggin Hill, Kent, where they remained for the winter. New Spitfire IXs were issued. On December 1, Charlie reported back to the squadron for operational duties. In the new location, the weather added to the men's woes. For the first 10 days of December, a blanket of fog shrouded the airport, making flying impossible. The fog lifted, but a heavy snowfall followed.

During the spring of 1944, the squadrons moved to Tangmere, where once again they were housed under canvas. Rumors circulated that an invasion could come at any time, and the pilots' training took on a new edge. They flew to Scotland for air firing courses and to Wales for armament practice. The airmen trained for a possible new role—dive-bombing—and carried out their first dive-bombing sortie against the Merville viaduct in April.

Finally, the day they had all been awaiting arrived—D-Day, June 6, 1944. The entire squadron was on readiness from first light, and most pilots had only two hours of sleep. The squadron flew four sweeps over the beachhead. Trainor flew aircraft *MJ 125* on patrols over Gold, Juno and Sword sectors. The pilots were disappointed that no enemy aircraft appeared, but the Canadian pilots were able to witness, with some satisfaction, the speed with which the ground forces secured their objective.

The squadron was on a continual state of enhanced readiness for the next week. The pilots were never far from their cockpits. Unable to sit down for regular meals, they were continuously provided with sandwiches, sweets, tea and coffee by the catering officers. On June 18, they had a half-hour notice to pack up and move across the English Channel to Airfield B4, located at Beny-sur-Mer in France. The dust kicked up by the landing aircraft soon turned to sticky mud the next day as the skies poured rain. Most of the men spent the time digging trenches inside their tents so they would not have to get up in the night if "Jerry decided to visit."

After weeks of little or no contact with the enemy, the squadron diary reported that June 28 was "the best in squadron history." The pilots carried out three operations, and on the last two, Trainor destroyed a Focke-Wulf 190 and a Messerschmitt 109.

Yellow Section, with Trainor in the number one position, was airborne at 1225 hours for an armed reconnaissance sortie. South and east of Caen, they attacked ground targets, leaving three enemy vehicles in flames and another four damaged. The pilots sighted 15 German fighters flying east, and Trainor singled out one Focke-Wulf 190 and chased him through puffs of cloud. He had to break off when two Messerschmitt 109s slipped in behind him and opened fire. He broke to the right, then back to the left to get behind the attacking pair. Charlie fired a half-second burst on one, who was 300 yards ahead of him. He saw no hits on the enemy plane, so he closed in to 250 yards and fired a second burst. This time, he hit the enemy, and many large pieces flew off his target. The German aircraft spun downwards and hit the ground. Trainor returned to base because he was running short of fuel.

Charlie took his refueled and rearmed Spitfire *MK 311* airborne again after dinner, at 1920 hours. He was again leading Yellow Section at 4000 feet northeast of Lisieux. The section encountered several enemy planes, and in one engagement, Trainor's airplane was hit by an attacking Focke-Wulf 190. He took strikes in the tail wheel and rear fuselage. Trainor rolled away and spotted another Focke-Wulf 190 flying alone through cloud. Charlie gave chase and, with only brief glimpses of the enemy through the cloud, got two bursts off after a pursuit of some 20 miles. He couldn't see if he had hit the other plane, but he flew through a puff of debris. When he came out of the cloud, no aircraft was in sight, but after a couple of orbits he saw an airplane burning fiercely on the ground.

The next day, June 29, Charlie was leading the entire squadron on a front line patrol at 7000 feet, five miles east of Caen. They took off at 1530 hours and had strafed a column of vehicles, damaging two. Trainor was in Spitfire *NH 341*, returning home with five squadron aircraft following him when 15 Messerschmitt 109s broke out of cloud and roared over their formation. Charlie broke left and got on the tail of one enemy, firing a short burst from about 150 yards. He saw many strikes,

Hugh Trainor happily poses by the wing of his 411 Squadron Spitfire in March 1944.

and pieces flew off the German machine, including the entire tail section. Flying Officer R.W. Hogg, flying as Charlie's wingman, saw a parachute at 2–3000 feet, apparently from the enemy aircraft. Charlie fired on another enemy, but he saw no hits before the aircraft entered the clouds.

Over the next two days, Charlie Trainor led Yellow Section, flying and fighting in the Caen area. On both days, he was again victorious over Messerschmitt 109s, destroying two more to bring his total to five, making him an ace. On July 3, the squadron diarist wrote: "Highlight today—F/L Trainor did NOT bag a Hun for the second successive day."

His luck returned on July 4 when he shot down two more Messerschmitt 109s. Then he and Squadron Leader Robertson were vectored by ground radar to investigate a bogey crossing the French coast two miles east of Cabourg. The bogey turned out to be a Dornier 217 bomber. Both the mid-upper gunner and the belly gunner shot at them, and Trainor and Robertson returned fire. Squadron members on the ground saw the enemy aircraft explode in the air. The two pilots shared the kill, and Trainor's score was now 7½.

On August 8, the *London Gazette* published Trainor's citation for a Distinguished Flying Cross:

> *"Within a very short period, Flight Lieutenant Trainor has shot down five enemy aircraft. His successes are a fine tribute to his great skill and fighting qualities."*

The citation confirmed Trainor's award of an immediate Distinguished Flying Cross on July 13. As well, Trainor had been appointed A Flight commander. The squadron diary noted, however, that it was over a month after D-Day and they were still eating iron rations (canned meals) instead of field rations. On July 26, Charlie was promoted to squadron leader and took command of No. 401 Squadron. The former commanding officer, Squadron Leader Hap Kennedy, had been hit by flak and forced to bail out. He was listed as missing.

His first day as commanding officer of the new squadron was "a lovely day and a great start for the squadron under its new management." The entire squadron got involved in a dogfight with 15 Messerschmitt 109s and Focke-Wulf 190s. Seven 109s and one 190 were destroyed. One of the victories belonged to Charlie Trainor. Another was Bill McRae's first victory after three scoreless years of combat flying. Four days later, on July 31, Trainor and Flight Lieutenant Klersy destroyed a Focke-Wulf 190 each in a fight with 12 of the enemy over Domfront.

With all the flying that the squadron was doing in support of the Allies' rapid advance, Charlie Trainor's luck was bound to run out. On August 18, he was leading his fliers on armed reconnaissance sorties against enemy transports fleeing from the Falaise pocket. The squadron flew 53 sorties, but on the first flight, Squadron Leader Trainor and Flying Officer C.E. Fairfield were hit by flak. Fairfield crashed and was killed. Trainor's aircraft was last seen heading south toward American lines.

Seven days later, on August 25, just about suppertime, Trainor walked onto his base. He had landed by parachute after he bailed out of his crippled Spitfire. Sympathetic French farmers, who had seen him descend, gave Trainor civilian clothes and hid him in a barn. He was eating supper with his benefactors one evening when a German officer tramped in and began asking questions. Wisely, Charlie kept his mouth shut and avoided detection.

Back at squadron, he took a short leave before returning to his command.

Early in September, the squadron had followed the fast-moving army into Belgium, and they were comfortably quartered on a former Luftwaffe airfield near Brussels. The base was a busy aerodrome, with many aircraft coming and going. Fresh supplies were brought in, and the food improved greatly; squadron members were even enjoying an egg each with their breakfast. The men were also basking in the pleasures of the city—hot baths, ice cream, wine, women and song.

On September 19, while flying in support of Operation Market Garden, the Allied push towards Germany, Charlie Trainor's engine developed fuel flow problems and quit at 23,000 feet. Charlie turned towards the Allied lines in hopes of gliding to safety. After sailing for about 20 miles, he bailed out. His wingmen followed his parachute down to about 500 feet before they lost sight of him in the ground haze. They were near the small town of Derwen but could not determine if the town was near Allied positions.

The squadron members kept their hopes up because " he walked out before and everyone is quite confident that he can repeat the performance." Not this time. On September 21, the squadron learned through the local underground resistance fighters that Trainor was a prisoner of war. He was captured after parachuting safely into the Netherlands. His captors stopped for a beer at a pub, but his guards were alert and the washroom window was far too small for Charlie to escape.

Squadron Leader Hugh Charles Trainor spent the rest of the war at Stalag Luft I in a small German town called Barth on the Baltic coast. The Russian Army liberated him in April 1945. Charlie was safely back in the United Kingdom by May 12 and arrived home in Canada on June 1. Trainor was officially released from the RCAF on October 4, 1945. His official wartime score was 8½ confirmed destroyed and one probably destroyed. Squadron Leader R.I.A. "Rod" Smith replaced Charlie as commanding officer of No. 401 Squadron.

Meanwhile, he had picked up a bar to his Distinguished Flying Cross and a Distinguished Service Order decoration:

"Since being awarded a bar to the Distinguished Flying Cross this officer has led the squadron on many sorties during which considerable success has been achieved. Within a period of three weeks some 385 enemy vehicles have been put out of action, many of them by Squadron Leader Trainor. In addition, 17 enemy aircraft were shot down, two of them by this gallant and relentless fighter. Throughout these operations Squadron Leader Trainor displayed magnificent leadership, great determination and devotion to duty."

After the war, Charlie Trainor flew as a commercial pilot for Maritime Central Airways and its successor, Eastern Provincial Airways. He married an airline stewardess, Imelda (Mel), and they had three children, sons Charles Jr. and James and daughter Ellen. Hugh Charles Trainor died at his home in Stratford, a suburb of Charlottetown, PEI, on July 4, 2004.

CHAPTER NINE

James Douglas "Doug" Lindsay
Tiger Moth to Sabre Jet
(1922–)

IN A CAREER THAT SPANNED 31 YEARS, DOUG LINDSAY FLEW two of the most important fighter aircraft in the inventory of the Royal Canadian Air Force—the Spitfire and the F86 Sabre. His skill as a fighter pilot is measured in his survival and his score. In World War II, he destroyed seven enemy aircraft in air-to-air battles and damaged five more. In Korea, he destroyed two Communist jets and damaged three.

James Douglas Lindsay was born on September 16, 1922, in the Ottawa Valley town of Arnprior, the son of Percy and Jessie (Watt) Lindsay. Percy had served in World War I as a company sergeant major with the 2nd Battalion and then worked for the E.B. Eddy Company managing woodlots. Growing up in bucolic Arnprior, Doug was a good student and an excellent athlete. He particularly enjoyed competing in track and field events. A teenaged friend who had his private pilot's licence introduced Doug to aviation when he took Doug flying in an Aeronca from the Arnprior flying club and even let Doug take the controls and fly. Doug had his first taste of the thrill of flight.

Doug had a year to go to complete high school when World War II broke out. As soon as he graduated school and turned 18, he travelled into Ottawa to enlist in the Royal Canadian Air Force on February 11, 1941. He was first sent to No. 3 Initial Training School to determine his fitness for aircrew. Selected to become a pilot, Doug was sent to No. 21 Elementary Flight Training School, where he would learn to fly on the Fleet Finch. He mastered flying the light airplane by September 1, 1941, and was sent on to No. 9 Service Flight Training School in Summerside, PEI. He learned to fly Yales and Harvards, which were both larger and faster than the Finch. Doug completed the ground school and flight training and graduated as a RCAF pilot on November 21, 1941. Because he finished in the top 10 of his class, Doug was commissioned as a pilot officer as well as earning his pilot's wings.

Instructor pilots were needed for the British Commonwealth Air Training Plan, and Doug's skill qualified him as a good instructor. He stayed in Canada to teach other fledgling aviators at Summerside, Uplands and Centralia. Despite his repeated pleas for an overseas posting, Doug did not get to England until February 1943. While he was preparing at the Operational Training Unit, Doug entered a half-mile race, and his fleet feet brought him in first.

Squadron Leader J.D. Lindsay, DFC and DFC (US), dressed in postwar flying gear as commander of 403 Squadron flying F86 Sabre jets from Bagotville, Québec.

On October 8, he reported for operational duties to No. 403 (Wolf) Squadron, flying the Spitfire IXC. That winter, the squadron flew routine patrols and bomber escort missions but had little contact with the enemy. In February, Doug was promoted to flight lieutenant.

On May 7, 1944, they were flying cover for some Bostons attacking locomotive shops at Valenciennes when a group of Messerschmitt 109s suddenly swirled in among them. Commonwealth fighter pilots knew that their Spitfires were as good or better than the German machines. The ensuing dogfight became a test of flying skill. Lindsay damaged one enemy aircraft and then caught another at low level. The second aircraft crashed under a hail of his bullets. At 21 years old, he had scored his first air-to-air victory. Back at base, he discovered his propeller had been dented from debris flying off the destroyed German plane.

On May 18, he was leading his section on a ground level sweep around Paris. In the strafing attack, they destroyed three motorcycles and a gasoline truck that exploded in a spectacular display of flame and smoke. A German staff car went into the ditch on fire, and another was forced to a halt with smoke pouring from its engine. On the road to Caen, they caught a large truck and left it in flames.

The days following D-Day were disappointing for Lindsay and the pilots of 403 Squadron. While other Canadian squadrons were engaging the enemy almost daily, the inactivity of the Wolf Squadron frustrated the airmen.

At last, on June 26, Doug and his section were on alert and scrambled to meet an incoming attack. Radar showed the intruders at low level, and the operators vectored the Canadians to intercept. Suddenly, the pilots were surrounded by 12 Messerschmitt 109s flying at 200 feet. As soon as the Spitfires attacked, the Germans broke away and climbed for the cloud layer at 1800 feet. Lindsay attacked one plane from astern and made several strikes, but he had to break off when at least six Focke-Wulf 190s entered the fray. The Germans made a firing pass then also climbed to escape in the cloud. The 403 pilots gave chase but lost them in the cloud. Reluctantly, they returned to base with a claim of one damaged Messerschmitt 109.

On the afternoon of June 29, Yellow Section, with Lindsay leading, was on an armed reconnaissance flight to the Bernay-Liagle-Argentan area. Radar control reported enemy aircraft in their area, and the section immediately climbed to 15,000 feet. Breaking through cloud, they saw at least 12 Focke-Wulf 190s in formation about eight miles away. The Canadians were maneuvering to get between the enemy and the sun (to attack with the light behind them) when their targets broke formation and dove for the protection of the clouds. The Canadians gave chase, and when they flew below the cloud, Lindsay saw a Focke-Wulf 190 shooting at a Spitfire. Doug dove on the enemy and opened up with all his guns blazing. He hit the German plane, and the Focke-Wulf began shedding pieces and exploded.

Four days later, on July 3, Doug's Yellow Section became involved in a melee of fighters all trying to knock each other from the sky. They were on a patrol over the Allied front lines east of Caen at 19,000 feet, just topping cloud, when they saw 15 Messerschmitt 109s. The Canadians dropped their auxiliary fuel tanks and turned to engage the enemy. Lindsay shot one with his 20-millimetre cannon. The pilot immediately ejected. Doug continued to overtake the formation and opened fire when another aircraft was caught in his gyro gun sight. The enemy tried to evade fire, but his right wing collapsed, and the Messerschmitt tumbled earthwards. In the diving and turning dogfight, Lindsay managed to get on the tail of another enemy fighter and maintained fire until the other machine blew up. Suddenly, the sky was empty, and the only sound Doug heard was his own engine. Twelve Spitfires had taken on 35 enemy aircraft of III/JG54 from Jagdkorps II without a second thought. They had destroyed six, probably destroyed another and damaged five without a single loss of their own.

This combat earned Doug Lindsay a Distinguished Flying Cross:

> *"This officer took part in an engagement against a large formation of enemy fighters, three of which he shot down. Flight Lieutenant Lindsay has invariably displayed praiseworthy courage and skill, and his keenness to engage the enemy has*

always been apparent. He has destroyed six enemy aircraft."

Lindsay ended his first tour on August 3, 1944. That last day, he destroyed a Messerschmitt 109 in a battle near Laigle and damaged another. He wangled a second tour with 403 during April 1945 and then went to 416 Squadron as flight commander of A Flight. The squadron commander was Squadron Leader J.D. Mitchner. On May 4, the day hostilities ended, Lindsay led four formations carrying 500-pound bombs on a shipping strike to Kiel Bay. The Allies wanted to thwart any enemy escape by sea. Seventeen of the bombs were near misses, one hit a ship just aft of the funnel, and another exploded on the hull of a 10,000-ton vessel.

Lindsay stayed in the RCAF postwar. He was promoted to squadron leader on January 1, 1950, and in 1951, he helped in the formation of No. 413 Squadron.

Doug went on exchange duties with the United States Air Force 39th Fighter Interceptor Squadron. Doug Lindsay went with the squadron to Korea on July 15, 1952. They flew the famed F-86 Sabre jet fighters against the Communists' Russian-made MIG-15s. On September 5, Lindsay damaged two MIGs, and on his 11th mission, on October 11, 1952, he destroyed an enemy aircraft. He damaged another Communist plane on October 25 and destroyed a second MIG on November 26.

Flying along the Yalu River near Kanggye, North Korea, Doug Lindsay and his wingman, USAF Lieutenant Harold Fischer, attacked a flight of 21 enemy aircraft at 46,000 feet. Two MIGs broke away from the formation, and the F-86s followed them in a climbing right turn. Lindsay fired on the lead MIG, and two more enemy aircraft joined the fight. Lindsay broke into the attackers and fired from 300 feet away. The pilot bailed out, and the MIG crashed. His wingman pulled in behind the other MIG and fired several bursts from 1200 feet, hitting its tail. The airplane crashed, and its pilot escaped by parachute.

The USAF awarded Squadron Leader Lindsay its Distinguished Flying Cross on May 8, 1953:

"Throughout his service with the Far East Command, [he] has displayed outstanding courage, aggressiveness and devotion to duty and has reflected great credit upon himself, the Royal Canadian Air Force and the United States Air Force."

Doug Lindsay came home on December 3, 1952, and was promoted to wing commander on January 1, 1953. Doug left the air force in 1972. He and his wife, Anne (Whelan), moved to Red Deer, Alberta, and took ownership of a Canadian Tire store. He finally retired to take up golf with his three sons, Robert, Graham and Michael, and dabble in watercolour painting.

CHAPTER TEN

John Alexander Kent
Kentowski
(1914–1985)

THE FIRST PHASE OF THE BATTLE OF BRITAIN RAGED ABOVE England from July 10 to August 18, 1940. The Luftwaffe was determined to cripple Britain's air defences, but a small band of gallant RAF airmen were just as determined that the German forces would not succeed. The most intense combat was from August 8 to 18, with a series of mass attacks designed to destroy the fighter forces of the RAF. German losses were two to one. The middle phase began on August 23, when huge formations of fighter-escorted bombers roared in night and day to blitz metropolitan centres. A ferocious climax came on September 15, when the Luftwaffe suffered its greatest losses. The final phase lasted until mid-October but consisted only of isolated hit-and-run attacks by high-flying fighters and bombers. By the end of October, the pressure was off—the RAF had won. Prime Minister Winston Churchill made his famous speech: "Never in the field of human conflict has so much been owed by so many to so few."

Canada played no small part in that epic battle. Canadian RAF and RCAF flyers in a dozen fighter squadrons, at least 18 bomber units and five Coastal Command squadrons were in action from the beginning. Most were Canadians flying with the RAF. The RCAF did not go into action until August 15, when Squadron Leader E.A. McNab of No. 1 Fighter Squadron, in a Hawker Hurricane, shot down a Dornier bomber over the Kent countryside. The RCAF had drawn first blood.

No. 1 Squadron was based at Northolt, Middlesex, where it flew and fought along side two other squadrons. One was No. 1 RAF Squadron. The other, No. 303 Polish Squadron RAF (mostly composed of Polish flyers) had a Canadian flight commander, Flight Lieutenant John A. Kent. Kent became a legend among legends. He destroyed 13 enemy aircraft in less than a year and on one occasion took on 40 German fighters single-handedly. His survival was nothing short of miraculous.

John Kent was born in Winnipeg on June 23, 1914. He was bitten by the flying bug early on. In 1929, for his 15th birthday, his father took him to the Winnipeg Flying Club for a ride in a Gypsy Moth. Two years later, his father began paying for flying lessons, and John was soon the youngest private pilot in Canada at age 17. Still not satisfied, John continued training until he gained his commercial flying licence in 1933, again as the youngest in Canada. Kent then looked for employment in the industry. Few jobs were available in

Flight Lieutenant J.A. Kent beside his 303 Squadron Hurricane.

commercial aviation, and the doors to the RCAF were closed because he did not have the minimum educational requirement—a university degree.

John's break came when he found an advertisement in a flying magazine offering young men a six-year short service commission in Britain's Royal Air Force. After four medical examinations and interviews in Winnipeg and long bureaucratic delays, he was invited to report to the British Air Ministry in London at his own expense. Once again his family provided the money, and John sailed for England in February 1935. He was accepted into the RAF and sent to No. 5 Flying Training School at Sealand to fly Avro Tutors for aircrew training. On February 29, 1936, he had a new set of pilot's wings on his chest, a pilot officer's thin stripe on each sleeve and his first posting, to No. 19 Squadron at Duxford for flying duties. Kent began flying Gloster Gauntlet biplane fighters, the best British fighter aircraft at the time. After an uneventful 18-month tour with the squadron, and two months' leave in Winnipeg, he was transferred for flight duties with the Royal Aircraft Establishment's experimental section at Farnborough as a test pilot. With the transfer came a promotion to flying officer.

Kent's job was to test aerial balloon-cable cutting devices. The scientists were testing the cable strengths for barrage balloon defences over Britain, and at the same time, by attaching blades to the nose of an aircraft, they were testing methods of cutting the balloon cables. The idea was to equip RAF planes with cutters, enabling them to slice through German defensive balloon arrays. The tests were exacting and dangerous. Flying at 7000 feet at speeds of 150 to 300 miles per hour, Kent would deliberately collide with the cables, causing varying degrees of damage to the aircraft. His proficiency and daring resulted in a commendation for the Air Force Cross. The recommendation was dated September 23, 1938:

> *"Flying Officer Kent has, during the last six months, made approximately 60 flights involving collision with a wire cable in connection with the special defence experiments carried out at this establishment. The experiment is one which is accompanied by a considerable element of risk to the pilot and calls for determination and a high degree of skill in piloting. Flying Officer Kent has at all times carried out these duties in a most efficient manner. He is fully aware of the nature of the risks he is taking but has never allowed this in any way to diminish the marked willingness and zeal with which he carried out these duties."*

That same month, John was promoted to flight lieutenant and received a permanent commission in the RAF. His future was assured. After three years of nerve-racking test pilot duties, on May 13, 1940, John went to Heston, joining the Photographic Development Unit. He flew photo-reconnaissance over France and Germany and earned the distinction of the first Canadian fighter pilot to experience anti-aircraft fire.

He was flying in his stripped-down Spitfire from the photo unit's airfield in France, 40 miles east of Paris. At 20,000 feet over the Rhine, he heard and felt a thumping that seemed to come from the tail of his aircraft. Checking the rearview mirror mounted above his head, he saw black and gray smoke puffs all around his airplane. Shocked, he realized that German flak was bursting all around him. He took evasive action, threw off the gunners' aim and rapidly completed his photo run before turning for home.

As the German army rolled over France, the unit was ordered to clear out. Kent and another pilot were the last to leave, escaping in two Tiger Moths. They were trundling down the runway when a formation of Junkers 88 bombers arrived overhead. Both pilots advanced their throttles. Just as they lifted off, the first German bombs hit the field. The two remained at treetop level, hoping that they were invisible to the bombers. The strategy worked, and they made their getaway.

In the early '40s, John Kent met and wed a Danish girl who was raised in Argentina. While he was off flying, she served as an officer in the Women's Auxiliary Air Force.

On July 27, 1940, Johnny Kent was posted to Northolt, 14 miles west of London, as a flight commander with the newly formed No. 303 Polish

Squadron. With the collapse of France, German occupation of Western Europe was complete. Polish pilots who had escaped came to England to continue their fight. They were keen fliers who fought splendidly, but they knew nothing of English aircraft and tactics or of the language. Kent was expected to teach them to fly the Hurricane and speak English. The Poles were impatient students. All they wanted to do was get up in the air and shoot down Germans. Kent won their respect and loyalty and the nickname "Kentowski." The men became skilled and ferocious fighters, establishing a splendid record for their squadron.

Johnny Kent scored his first combat victory on September 9, 1940. He was leading a formation of his Poles and Canadians from No. 1 Fighter Squadron over the Channel near Beachy Head. They encountered 40 Junkers 88 bombers escorted by a flock of fighters. Kent dove on a straggling bomber with his eight machine guns blazing. The bomber ducked into the cloud cover. Kent followed with three Messerschmitt 109s chasing him. Emerging from the overcast, the Allied pilots lost sight of their intended victim but noticed a lone Messerschmitt 110. Kent led his section in behind the enemy, and the German rear cockpit gunner opened fire on the Hurricanes. Kent later recalled, "It was quite fascinating and made a pretty sight in the gloom watching my tracers sail gracefully towards the German while at the same time his came streaming back at me like a string of gleaming beads." Kent's bullets silenced the enemy gunner and set the aircraft's starboard engine and wing on fire. The German plane made a gentle turn but then dove into the water. John was credited with a destroyed fighter, his first successful air combat, and a damaged bomber—the Junkers 88.

The Battle of Britain raged on in English skies, and the Polish squadron was in the thick of it. Continually taking off, fighting, refuelling and taking off again was exhausting work. While on alert status, wearing bright yellow Mae West life-preservers over their blue uniforms, the pilots lounged about their dispersal huts smoking, dozing, chatting, playing cards, writing letters—killing time. But under that outward display of calm lay an inner nervousness, an itching for action to which they would instantly respond once the signal came to scramble—take off on the double and intercept the enemy. With the help of their ground crews, who stood by their Hawker Hurricane or Supermarine Spitfire fighter planes, the pilots had the drill down cold.

Arthur Bishop, a veteran of No. 1 (later 401) Fighter Squadron's exploits, described what it was like to be scrambled:

> *"When the order came they would dash to their aircraft while pulling on their parachute seat packs, climb up on the port wing root and lower themselves into the cockpit. Then donning their leather flying helmets that dangled from the control column, they would plug their facemasks into the radio transmitter, which would simultaneously*

connect them to the oxygen feed. Next step, pull down the goggles strapped to the helmet. That accomplished they would "press tits" [punch ignition buttons with index and forefingers] *bringing the Rolls-Royce Merlin engine to life while the "erks"* [ground crews] *secured their safety straps. From the time the phone jangled and the Klaxon horn began its mournful wail, they could be airborne within three minutes. In pilot's lexicon, 'A piece of cake!'"*

His next success occurred mid-morning on September 23. He destroyed a Messerschmitt 109 and damaged a Focke-Wulf 58. His battle with the Messerschmitt was memorable. The two aviators wheeled and dived in a tight air battle ballet. Time and again, Kent poured bullets into his opponent, but the enemy stubbornly refused to break off. After a terrific pounding, part of the German's tailplane and cockpit canopy broke away. Before Kent could fire again, the Messerschmitt lazily rolled over, and the pilot bailed out over the Channel.

On his way back to the coast, John saw an aircraft like nothing he had ever seen before. He pulled up close for a better look and saw the black crosses on the wings. It was the enemy. Getting into firing position, Kent raked the length of the aircraft's fuselage. The unknown airplane stayed airborne and did not return fire. Kent's ammunition was low, and he broke off to return to base. Intelligence officers later identified the Focke-Wulf 58, an aircraft rarely seen.

No. 303 Squadron was the top-scoring unit in Fighter Command, with 108 enemies claimed as destroyed. Kent adopted a personal emblem for his aircraft—a green maple leaf emblazoned with a white Polish eagle.

On October 1, Kent engaged in his most spectacular air battle. In mid-afternoon the wing was scrambled to meet a large formation approaching England's coast. At 10,000 feet, Johnny spotted the intruding bombers. Moving into an attack position, he drew far ahead of his section. The Canadians flying with him were bounced by fighters and had to break in the opposite direction. Suddenly Kent found himself very much alone in the middle of a hornet's nest of Messerschmitt 109s.

His only advantage was that every aircraft that flew into his sights was a valid target. A section of four Messerschmitts banked in front of him. A quick burst sent one enemy spinning down, leaving a trail of smoke. Another appeared 50 yards in front of him, and his bullets quickly caused it to burst into flames and disappear. Kent got below the belly of the German leader, striking the enemy all along its fuselage. Probably low on fuel, the remaining fighters hightailed it for France. The brash Canadian chased them and counted 38 aircraft. Counting the two he had hit, his blood ran cold as he realized he had just single-handedly fought off 40 German planes. On the way home, he saw a single Messerschmitt 109 headed for the Continent. He fired the last of his ammunition, and the enemy dove into a cloud to hide. On the ground, John discovered that he had escaped without a scratch. There was not a single bullet hole in his Hurricane.

His award of the Distinguished Flying Cross on October 25, 1940, cited:

"...when entirely alone, [he] attacked 40 Messerschmitt 109s and shot down two of them. He has personally destroyed at least four enemy aircraft. Flight Lieutenant Kent has been responsible in a large measure for the fighting efficiency of his squadron and has materially contributed to its successes. He has proven himself a born leader."

As well as receiving the Distinguished Flying Cross, Kent was promoted to squadron leader and sent to take command of No. 92 Squadron. In the first two days of November, he celebrated his promotion by shooting down three aircraft and probably destroying a fourth, all in a space of five minutes. To Johnny, the first one seemed to take forever. They fought and rolled and fought some more. Speaking to an interviewer in 1941, he said:

"The first one fought too well. Eventually he went down but not before I thought he was going on forever. I found out later he was a German major with a long string of decorations, but I never learned his name."

In January 1941, No. 92 Squadron moved to Manston. Kent took over what he called a "disorganized, undisciplined and demoralized collection of first class material." The squadron had suffered dreadful losses and had been through four commanding officers in the previous month. Kent's leadership skills soon had the pilots flying and fighting like the first class material they were. A personal highlight for John was his award of the Order of Virtuti Militari by the Polish government in exile, one of their country's highest decorations.

In March 1941, John Kent was appointed chief flying instructor at No. 53 Operational Training Unit in Heston and was promoted to wing commander.

Three months later, he was posted back to Northolt as the wing commander (flying), with command of all three Polish squadrons, Nos. 303, 306 and 308. Now the men were flying on the French side of the Channel, and Kent personally kept the standard high by destroying four more Messerschmitt 109s—one each day—on June 21 west of St. Omer, June 27 while strafing a German airfield, July 3 and July 20.

On August 2, Wing Commander John Kent assumed command of a fighter wing at Kenley. He got two more Messerschmitt 109s in August, one on the 7th, again in the St. Omer area, and the other on the 15th over the sand dunes of Gravelines. While at Kenley Wing, he was awarded the bar to his Distinguished Flying Cross on October 21, 1941:

"This officer has led his wing in an efficient and fearless manner on many operational sorties

within the last two months. He has destroyed a further six enemy aircraft, bringing his total success to 13 destroyed and three probably destroyed. Wing Commander Kent has set a grand example."

He was 27 years old.

Early in 1942, Johnny Kent was taken off operational duties and went on a North American lecture tour. On his return, he was given command of RAF Station Church Fenton, which housed Nos. 310 and 313 Czech Fighter Squadrons.

In December 1942, he went to the Mediterranean to command No. 17 (Benghazi) Sector until August 1943 when he took over No. 234 Wing. Still not content to fly a desk, he was often in the air. Once, he was flying an old Hurricane when radar asked him to check out a bogey. It turned out to be a Junkers 88 prowling 15 miles northeast of Tolmeita Cyrenacca. Before his cannons quit, he had damaged the bomber by setting an engine on fire. With no ammunition left, he had to let the airplane escape. It was his last air combat.

He returned to England in March 1944 and took command of No. 7 Flying Instructors School followed by No. 3 Advanced Flying Unit. Postwar, Kent was appointed personal staff officer to Air Chief Marshal Sir Sholto Douglas, the military governor of British-occupied Germany and commander of the British Air Forces of Occupation.

W/C John "Kentowski" Kent (left) and another officer.

In 1947, he returned to duties as the chief test pilot at Farnborough, England. Kent followed that with a tour as an exchange officer in the flight and all-weather test division of the USAF at Wright-Patterson Air Force Base in Dayton, Ohio. In 1952, John was given command of RAF Station Odiham and promoted to group captain.

In December 1956, he retired from the air force, and in June 1957 took a position as a sales manager for Kelvin and Hughes (Aviation) Ltd., an aviation electronics firm. He had flown 217 different types of aircraft during his career, but nothing excited him as much as flying with the fearless Poles of No. 303 Squadron. Their spirit and courage matched his own.

Group Commander (retired) John Alexander Kent died on October 7, 1985, at his home in Hartley Wintney, Hants.

CHAPTER ELEVEN

John Davidson Mitchner
Fighter Ace and Dive Bomber
(1914–1964)

JOHN MITCHNER JOINED NO. 402 SQUADRON AT KENLEY ON November 17, 1942. He flew his Spitfire IXC on a number of day patrols, fighter sweeps and bomber escorts before engaging in air-to-air combat with Luftwaffe fighters. At the time, the German flyers avoided mixing it up with the Spitfires. As a junior pilot, Mitchner primarily flew as a wing-man to a more experienced flyer. The wingman's job was to look and learn, but most importantly, he was expected to follow his leader into action and keep enemy aircraft off the other pilot's tail. On January 17, 1943, Mitchner claimed a damaged Focke-Wulf 190 after a strafing attack on the German airfield at Bolbec, east of Le Havre, one of six aircraft damaged by squadron pilots on that flight. The sortie was a costly raid for the Canadians; they lost three pilots, including Red Section leader Wing Commander F.J. Fee, commander of the Canadian wing at Kenley, and one of Fee's wing-men. But it was not until John's 57th sortie, on July 27, that he claimed an enemy destroyed.

That warm summer day, 402 Squadron set out on a ramrod operation, escorting a dozen USAF

Mitchell bombers on a raid to Schipol airport in the Netherlands. As they approached the target, a group of 30 to 45 enemy fighters tried to halt the bombers. A tremendous dogfight broke out. Mitchner, flying as number three in Yellow Section, shot up an enemy Messerschmitt 109. His target trailed smoke and glycol as it rolled over and plummeted toward the ground. Pilot Officer Mitchner followed him down. At about 1500 feet, as the 109 pilot tried to pull his aircraft out of the dive, Mitchner let loose another stream from his machine guns. The hood and another piece of the Messerschmitt's cockpit flew off as the gravely damaged airplane plunged into the sandy beach. Mitchner had his first combat victory.

The rest of the summer was mainly bloodless, but John broke the pattern with four victories in September. That autumn began a string of successful sorties that would only end after Mitchner had completed two tours of operations, flown 233 sorties (by his own count) and destroyed 10½ enemy aircraft. He was honoured with two Canadian decorations and one from the Netherlands for his skill in the air and his devotion to duty.

John Davidson Mitchner was born in Saskatoon on July 3, 1914. He grew up and completed his education in the Prairie city, becoming a bookkeeper. Both the Boy Scouts and membership in

Squadron Leader J.D. Mitchner, DFC & Bar.

the YMCA moulded his character. John went to Vancouver as a bookkeeper and salesman for a fuel oil company. At age 26, he enlisted as an aircraftsman second class on October 26, 1940, and was sent to No. 2 Manning Depot in Brandon, Manitoba, for basic training and selection for aircrew. After successfully learning to march and wear the air force uniform, he was sent on guard duties to No. 4 Service Flight Training School in Saskatoon. This fortuitous posting meant that he would spend his first Christmas in uniform at home.

On January 5, 1941, John Mitchner reported to No. 2 Initial Training School in Regina. His success at the course led to a promotion to leading aircraftsman and flight training at No. 8 Elementary Flight Training School in Vancouver. Pilots trained at the Aero Club of BC; John's first flying was in a Tiger Moth under the guidance of civilian instructors. On April 10, John joined a flying course at No. 10 Service Flight Training School in Dauphin, Manitoba. He began his service flying the bright yellow Harvard. The speed, maneuverability and sheer weight of the Harvard were a complete change from the nimble Tiger Moth. Mitchner's performance was only mediocre. The only noteworthy incidence was when he stood a Tiger Moth on its nose when he applied the brakes too forcefully while taxiing. After completing his lessons, on July 8, 1941, John stood proud on parade to accept the coveted wings and a simultaneous promotion to sergeant. He felt more than ready to take on the Luftwaffe in operational flying. He was sent to the depot in Halifax to await a ship for the United Kingdom.

Sergeant pilot Mitchner arrived at the Personnel Reception Centre in Bournemouth, England, on August 16, 1941. Posted to No. 263 (RAF) Squadron at Charmy Down near Bath, Mitchner was introduced to the twin-engine Whirlwind. He flew several uneventful convoy patrols from September 1941 until June 1942. At the same time, he was slowly progressing up through the ranks. Mitchner was promoted to flight sergeant on December 22, 1941, and then warrant officer second class on June 22, 1942. He was upgraded to warrant officer first class on July 1, 1942.

In June, he joined about 15 other Canadians at No. 55 Fighter Operational Training Unit, flying the famous Hawker Hurricanes. Training wrapped up on July 16, 1942, and John went to No. 247 (RAF) Squadron where he continued to fly Mk X Hurricanes. Routine convoy patrols dominated his flying time. He returned from one patrol on July 30, 1942, and landed far too fast, overshooting the airfield and ploughing through a fence. He was uninjured, but the aircraft wasn't so lucky. Shuttled off through No.116 Squadron, John Mitchner finally arrived at No. 402 (City of Winnipeg) Squadron, based with the Canadian Wing at Kenley, on November 17,1942.

That winter, the 402 pilots spent most of their time trying to intercept German fighter-bombers that swooped in on low-level attacks along the English coast. Mitchner celebrated the New Year with the news that he was to be offered his commission. On January 12, 1943, he donned his tailored officer's uniform with the thin stripe of a pilot officer on the sleeve. The squadron was flying escort sorties, protecting formations of light bombers en route to targets in France and the Netherlands. Along with No. 416 Squadron, No. 402 moved to Digby to form a new Canadian wing in March 1943.

Mitchner's first success was on July 27, two weeks after he was promoted to flying officer. By September he was a flight lieutenant and A Flight commander. He engaged and destroyed or damaged five enemy aircraft. On September 4, while escorting Marauders over St. Pol, he shot down a Messerschmitt 109 and then got another one on September 8. One bomber was lost, but it was to flak and not to enemy fighters. On September 24, more than 40 enemy fighters attacked the escorts. Wing Commander Chadburn, commanding officer of Digby Wing, shared one destroyed Focke-Wulf 190 with Mitchner, and later in the same action, Chadburn and Mitchner shared a probably destroyed enemy with Sergeant Thorne, an American flying in the RCAF.

Three days later, on September 27, the wing was protecting 36 USAAF Marauders on a bombing sortie to German airfields in northern France when 10 or so Focke-Wulf 190s dove to attack. The squadron broke formation to meet the German planes. Mitchner saw an enemy sliding in behind Chadburn, and he and Pilot Officer Innes turned to meet the threat. Both Canadians fired and saw their cannon shells tear up the 190's fuselage. Their target disappeared into the clouds, and the pair could not conclusively determine its fate. They were both credited with a probably destroyed. Moments later, Chadburn radioed to warn Mitchner of two enemy aircraft trying to catch them. He told Mitchner to lead the section straight on so Chadburn could get in firing position without the 190s knowing they had been detected. John's discipline to hold his course and his trust that his fellow pilot would protect him could not be more evident. The wing commander opened fire with cannons and machine guns, shooting down one aircraft and probably destroying the other.

On October 3, the squadron flew to Coltishall (near the Norfolk coast) and resumed flying close escort for Marauders attacking Schipol airport. The bombing results were excellent, but the fighters met with considerable enemy opposition. Uncomfortably accurate heavy flak added to their woes. Mitchner was credited with damaging one of the attacking Messerschmitt 109s. The squadron's escort duties continued, but the Luftwaffe had pulled back from aggressively meeting Allied fighters. The fighter pilots of Jagdkorps II were totally incapable of posing any effective challenge to Allied air supremacy because of the Germans' shortage of leaders and poor training of replacement pilots. The commanding general complained to Generalfeldmarschall Sperrle about the absence of German fighters over the front.

The pilots were flying two or three sorties each week, but enemy aircraft rarely engaged them. Flying became so mundane that the pilots amused themselves in January by holding a mustache-growing contest. For some of the squadron's young warriors, growing facial hair was a challenge.

After flying 127 sorties, Mitchner was posted to No. 9 Group at RAF Station Tealing for flight instructor duties on February 22, 1944. The 402 Squadron Operational Record noted: "'Mitch' is another old member of the squadron and has done very good work during the months of his tour."

Mitchner had been awarded the Distinguished Flying Cross on November 9 for having:

> "... completed a large number of sorties against the enemy including several very successful attacks on shipping, He is a most determined and able leader whose confidence in action has proved inspiring in combat. Flight Lieutenant Mitchner has destroyed three enemy aircraft."

The reference to shipping acknowledged his action with his wingman off the Dutch coast. They were on a shipping reconnaissance sortie and decided to go low level and strafe what they saw. They scored on a barge, a 2000-ton steamer and a ferry. The citation failed to mention that in the same time frame he had damaged three enemy aircraft, probably destroyed one and shared in the probable destruction of two more.

In August 1944, John Mitchner was sent to join
No. 421 (Red Indian) Squadron at Brazenville in
Normandy, supporting the ground troops in the
Battle of Falaise. Their daily role was to roar over
the battlefield at low level looking to put enemy
vehicles out of action. On these armed reconnaissance sorties, the pilots became the scourge of the
retreating German army. Suddenly appearing
low over the roads and fields, they hammered
armoured vehicles, trucks, tanks, staff cars and
mechanized and horse-drawn artillery leaving
a scrapyard full of "flamers" (burning vehicles),
"smokers" (equipment smoking but not in flames)
and damaged vehicles.

Shortly after noon on August 23, two days
before the liberation of Paris, 18 II/JG26 Focke-
Wulf 190s and five III/JG26 Messerschmitt 109s
joined a gaggle of over 60 German fighters to attack
24 Spitfires of No.127 Wing (RCAF). The battle
split up into individual dogfights, and the Spitfires
were greatly outnumbered. The wing claimed
12 German fighters and a loss of three Spitfires, but
II/JG26 claimed the destruction of six Spitfires.

Late in September, the air forces turned their
attention to the area around Nijmegen in the
Netherlands. The Luftwaffe was active again, usually trying to reach the advancing Allied troops for
strafing attacks. On the ground, Operation Market
Garden was in full swing. The objective was to
seize a corridor to the Rhine and establish a bridgehead over the river. To avoid the possibility of

firing on friendly forces, 2nd Tactical Air Force was prohibited from attacking targets of opportunity unless fired upon first. Complicating coordination was the problem that there was no way for the airmen to communicate with the soldiers. Meanwhile, the Luftwaffe had made a remarkable recovery and was trying to destroy the bridges at Eindhoven and Nijmegen.

Mitchner joined No. 421 on August 13 and flew armed reconnaissance sorties on the 15th and 18th. On his second sortie, the squadron met accurate and intense light flak but still left behind six flamers, 27 smokers and 18 damaged motorized enemy transports. On September 22, the wing moved to Beauvechain, Belgium, where the 421 pilots were housed in German barracks that looked "like a sieve due to blast effect." The weather didn't help much, turning miserably cold and rainy. On the afternoon of September 25, No. 421 ran into a gaggle of a dozen German aircraft. Mitchner, flying Spitfire *MK 232*, lined up a Messerschmitt 109, which promptly dove from 7000 feet to 3000 feet. The Canadian pulled a tight turn inside the German's orbit and put a stream of fire into the Messerschmitt's cockpit. The pilot bailed out.

Rejoining his section at 12,000 feet, he spotted a Focke-Wulf 190 below and dove to attack. The 190 scampered into the cloud layer at 6000 feet. Mitchner followed and throttled back as he entered

S/L J.D. Mitchner, DFC & Bar, leads a Spitfire squadron at an airfield in Belgium.

the mist. Emerging, he found himself flying along-side the Focke-Wulf. The German had cut his power hoping that the Spitfire would overshoot and present a target. Instead, Mitchner swung in behind his prey. One long burst did the trick; the 190 caught fire and exploded.

Two days later, again in Spitfire *MK 232*, they engaged six Messerschmitt 109s in the Nijmegen area. A silver enemy aircraft with checkered cowlings was Mitchner's last encounter with the foe when he was flying with 421 Squadron. On September 28, he was transferred to No. 416 (City of Oshawa) Squadron at Le Culot as B Flight commander. Commanding No. 416 Squadron was another Canadian ace, Squadron Leader John F. McElroy. The day after Mitchner arrived, the squadron moved to Grave, Netherlands.

On his first sortie with No. 416, about noon on September 29, Jake Mitchner was leading a formation of 11 Spitfires on the usual low-level patrol over Nijmegen when ground control radar vectored them towards a dogfight in progress over Emmerich to the east. They found some Allied Tempests tangling with more than 20 Focke-Wulf 190s. Mitchner, leading Green Section, tried to get into position to attack two of them, but a third got on his tail and forced him to break away. He quickly rolled astern of his pursuer, fired a short burst, and the enemy went down in flames. A second aircraft soon followed. The German jettisoned his canopy hood and leapt from his smoke-filled cockpit.

In September 1944, Jagdgeschwader 26 claimed a victory total of 66 with a loss of 31 (27 pilots killed in action, one killed in an accident and three taken prisoners). Their efforts could have no effect on the course of the war.

Unexpectedly, the Luftwaffe left the skies to Allied aircraft. The squadron reverted to low-level patrols looking for enemy transports to shoot up. On October 29, Mitchner received his promotion to squadron leader and confirmation that he would take command of the squadron when tour-expired McElroy left at the end of the month.

Throughout November, the squadron pilots wondered if Germany still had an air force. They had hardly seen a single aircraft since arriving in the Netherlands. On Armistice Day, November 11, the squadron historian commented, "Too bad history cannot repeat itself." All the pilots not on duty were on parade in Brussels in the pouring rain, taking time to honour the troops of World War I even in the middle of another war.

While leading the squadron on December 8, Mitchner, in Spitfire *MJ 815*, racked up his last aerial victory. The pilots were flying a fighter sweep near the city of Münster when Mitchner destroyed one of three enemy Messerschmitt 109s found flying at 12,000 feet. The remaining pilots still lamented the lack of Germans in the air. They flew uneventful escort sorties, dive-bombing attacks on ground targets and armed reconnaissance flights. Also flying with No. 416 Squadron was another Canadian ace, Flight Lieutenant J.D. Lindsay, who eventually took over A Flight.

On March 5, Squadron Leader Mitchner cracked open a bottle of Scotch to celebrate his award of the Netherlands Flying Cross, "in recognition of valuable services rendered during the heavy fighting around Arnhem and Nijmegen."

On April 30, Mitchner led an armed reconnaissance mission east of the Elbe River around Schwerin, Germany. The Canadians caught a column of over 100 vehicles and strafed it from end to end. As they flew away, they left 13 motorized enemy transports in flames and 63 damaged. Leading another sortie the same day, the airmen found vehicles parked along the side of a road in some woods. They hit every one, leaving 15 destroyed and 13 damaged. Continuing the patrol, they damaged five goods trucks and two locomotives despite heavy flak from one rail car. To complete their day, they strafed a barn in which German troops were hiding. The attacks were dangerous work, and many pilots were lost, but Mitchner was never once hit by enemy fire.

Mitchner's devotion to duty, determination and able leadership was recognized in the last weeks of the war with a bar to his Distinguished Flying Cross: "He has been responsible for the destruction of 10 enemy aircraft." He destroyed four enemies and shared in one kill with 402 Squadron in 1943, took down three with 421 Squadron in September 1944 and destroyed three more while leading 416 Squadron.

On May 4, 1945, the news of Germany's surrender reached the squadron. Celebrations were subdued. For most of the men, their big day would come when they climbed aboard a ship home. On VE Day, many of the pilots were away at German aerodromes to fly Luftwaffe aircraft to Allied airfields.

For the rest of May, pilots flew formation flypasts over German cities such as Bremerhaven, List and Kiel-Schleswig-Hohn. Mitchner officially kept command of 416 Squadron until January 15, 1946, and was repatriated to Canada on March 31.

Squadron Leader John Mitchner elected to remain in the postwar RCAF. He took command of No. 417 (Fighter Reconnaissance) Squadron at Rivers, Manitoba, on May 23, 1947, and stayed until January 20, 1949. He attended Staff College in Toronto for a year and was promoted to wing commander on September 1, 1951. His next challenge was the re-formation of No. 434 (Bluenose) Squadron as a day-fighter unit, flying the North American F86 Sabre jet. He took command of the squadron, based at Uplands (Ottawa), Ontario, on June 7, 1952, and relinquished command on February 21, 1953, just as the squadron was heading to Zweibrucken, Germany, to join No. 3 Fighter Wing.

In 1953, he discovered he had diabetes and was permanently grounded. He commanded two Cold War radar sites, St. Sylvestre and Lac St. Denis, but was released on medical grounds on November 27, 1964. He and his wife retired to the Okanagan region of British Columbia where he died in Penticton on December 2, 1964. He left his widow and three children.

CHAPTER TWELVE

Roderick Illingsworth Alpine "Rod" Smith

Top Gun
(1922–2002)

WHEN ROD SMITH HAD HIS ROYAL CANADIAN AIR FORCE pilot's wings pinned on, it was truly his childhood dream come true. Growing up in Regina, he spent every available moment when he was not at school or delivering newspapers at the airport watching airplanes take off and land. He and his brother Jerrold (Jerry) built flyable model aircraft with operating gas engines. They often hid aviation magazines in their schoolbooks. Both boys knew they wanted to be fighter pilots, and they built their whole lives around that dream. The two planned to go to England to join the Royal Air Force.

Rod was born to Donald Alpine Smith and Blanche (Robertshaw) Smith in Regina on March 21, 1922. Jerry was almost a year older. The boys' father was a veteran of the Canadian Expeditionary Force of World War I and had become a civil engineer and land surveyor in civilian life. During his high school years Rod participated in sports including hockey, baseball and tennis, but his main love was swimming.

Squadron Leader R.I.A. Smith, DFC and Bar.

He was an active participant in the local Sea Cadet corps. When war broke out, he still had a year to go to complete high school. That done, on September 30, 1940, Rod enlisted in the Royal Canadian Air Force. A month later, Jerry followed him, and the brothers' flying careers took divergent paths for a short while.

Rod began his service at No. 2 Manning Depot in Brandon, Manitoba. With basic training complete, he went on to the No. 2 Initial Training School back home in Regina. With an aptitude for pilot training, Rod entered the British Commonwealth Air Training Plan and went on to No. 2 Elementary Flight Training School at Fort William, Ontario. The civilian instructors of the Thunder Bay Flying Club taught him to fly Tiger Moths. Once he had mastered the rudimentary skills of piloting he was posted to No. 2 Service Flight Training School at Uplands (Ottawa), Ontario. Air force instructors took over and taught Rod the complexities of the Harvard and the Yale. The young pilot threw himself completely into aviation and achieved a distinguished pass. He graduated eighth in his class of 44 students.

Usually, pilots receiving their wings at a service flight training school were promoted from leading aircraftsman to sergeant. However, those who excelled on their flight tests and written examinations and demonstrated maturity and leadership skills were offered a commission with their wings. Throughout the war, the RCAF fought to have all aircrew commissioned, but RAF senior officers successfully thwarted every attempt. The RAF also maintained a ban on fraternization between non-commissioned and commissioned pilots—a ban more often ignored than obeyed by Canadians. After performing so well in training, Rod was made a pilot officer and given orders for overseas service. He received his wings on March 18, 1941, and on April 14, he embarked aboard the cruiser *California* for the two-week voyage to the United Kingdom.

Rod had long admired the clean lines and the power of the Spitfire. To him, it was the ultimate aircraft, so when he was assigned to a Spitfire Operational Training Unit at Grangemouth, Scotland, he was living his flying fantasy. Even folding his six-foot-three-inch frame into the Spitfire's cramped cockpit (smallest of all the fighters) did not deter him. He spent every available moment in the air. There were no dual-controlled Spitfires, so the new pilot was shown the appropriate switches, knobs and dials and was sent to try them out. His first flight in the Spitfire was his first solo. Once again Rod excelled, graduating at the top of his class. On June 23, 1941, he joined his first operational squadron, No. 412 (Falcon) Squadron.

Many of the great aviators of World War I were lone wolves who liked to fight alone. But such fighters were rare in World War II. Faster aircraft and higher altitudes meant that the pilots flew as teams rather than individuals. The favoured fighter formation was called the finger four. It resembled the fingers of a hand, with the leader flying as the foremost fingertip. Several variations were flown, but the basic rule was "Don't break formation!" The leader led the attack, and the wingman's primary job was to cover his backside. However, once a dogfight broke out, it was every man for himself until the leader called for the formation to regroup.

No. 412 Squadron was one of the new 400 series Canadian squadrons. Its Spitfire pilots spent most of the summer working up to operational standards, and Rod did not fly his first combat sortie until September, patrolling the English Channel over a convoy. Occasionally, the squadron flew a fighter sweep over northern France, which was much more dangerous and exciting than convoy patrols. On March 18, 1942, Rod Smith was promoted to flying officer, although he did not learn of it until May, just before he left for Malta.

On July 15, 1942, Rod flew his Spitfire off the Royal Navy aircraft carrier *Eagle*, bound for Malta's RAF Station Luqa. He had never taken off from the deck of an aircraft carrier before, and there was little option to return. Pilots were told if they ran into mechanical problems, they were to ditch into the sea rather than attempt to land on the ship. The flight was his longest flight in a Spitfire—three hours—and the hot dusty airfield was less than inviting. German bombers regularly blew holes in the runway and adjacent grounds. But any land looked good to Rod, who had squeezed his lanky body into the small, uncomfortable, uncushioned seat of the fighter.

His welcome to No. 126 RAF Squadron was enhanced with the news that brother Jerry had arrived just a week earlier. Jerry had flown off the

USS *Wasp* on May 17, but in contravention of his orders, when his fuel feed threatened engine failure, he returned and landed without arrester cables to stop him. The feat impressed U.S. naval officers who arranged a ride in a B-24 the next day from Gibraltar to Malta. Jerry had already flown operations with No. 126 Squadron, and the brothers were teamed up in the same flight, with Jerry leading and Rod flying as number two.

No. 126 Squadron flew Spitfires defending Malta against German and Italian air force attacks from Sicily. Malta was crucial to the progress of the German and Italian offensive in the African Western Desert. The island dominated the sea routes from Gibraltar to Italy, and the Axis was determined to blockade it to deny food, fuel and ammunition to the defenders. The Allied troops' only protection came from day and night fighters that fought tenaciously to hold air superiority. The air war was so continuous and so intense that many Canadians became aces over Malta. The pilots who survived went on to become flight, squadron and wing commanders in Europe.

Rod and Jerry were flying together on July 18 when they spotted a Junkers 88 heading to Sicily. In attack position, Jerry opened fire and then broke away so Rod could also open up. The Junkers' starboard engine began streaming smoke and glycol. Rod's cannons quit, and both aircraft were running low on fuel, so the brothers had to head home. The enemy plane was last seen limping low above the waves with its tail down. The brothers were credited with a probable destroyed.

The Smiths were teamed again on July 24 and scrambled to meet a wave of enemy bombers escorted by Messerschmitt 109s. They raced to 18,000 feet then dove to attack five Junkers bombers. Rod hit his target with a six-second burst that set the fuselage and port engine on fire. One crewmember bailed out as the bomber plunged to earth. The plane crashed and blew up just south of the Luqa airfield. Jerry also destroyed a bomber but was hit by one of its escorts. Rod covered his brother as Jerry glided back to base and made his landing without power. This action was Rod's first victory and raised Jerry's score to three.

Two days later, they dove through a cloud of Messerschmitt 109s to get at eight Junkers. Rod's bullets missed, but Jerry damaged one bomber before he was hit again. With Luqa being bombed, they had to land at the alternate field, Halfar.

On July 28, seven Spitfires bounced three enemy bombers and shot them all down. Rod fired a series of short bursts that set the enemy alight. The bomber dove downward, losing both engines, and its wings fell off. Rod had his second kill. Jerry, with a bullet hole in his glycol system, had to make his third forced landing in six days.

On August 10, Jerry made his last flight. The brothers were on 30-minute readiness, but both needed the silk glove liners for their leather gauntlets. Rod took a motorcycle to the supply section, half a mile away. In his absence, the section was ordered to their cockpits, and another airman had to take Rod's place. There was no time to switch before takeoff. The Spitfires roared down the runway and climbed away. Jerry never came back. He outdistanced his wingmen and intercepted the enemy alone. There were reports of a parachute, but his body was never recovered. The brothers were finally separated by death.

Rod grieved, but he knew he had to concentrate on the business at hand or he too might greet death in the air. On August 13, he was flying a convoy patrol and shot down a plane that was threatening the tanker *Ohio*—the Italian triple-engine Savoia-Marchetti 79 was a particularly dangerous torpedo bomber.

In September, Rod developed sandfly fever, a viral infection contracted from the bites of sandflies. It produces flu-like symptoms of headaches and general malaise. On top of that, he had a bad bout of sinusitis. After a few weeks he recovered, just in time to meet the threat of the October blitz. German and Italian bombers pounded Malta with as many explosives as were dropped on Britain during its blitz. The fighters spent most of the month scrambling to fend off enemy bombers.

On October 11, the squadron scrambled to meet nine incoming Junkers bombers covered by

60 Messerschmitt 109s. Leading Blue Section, Smith ascended to just astern the left-hand bomber. Rod opened fire at 250 yards. The enemy's engines caught fire, and the Junkers dived away. One of the crewmen bailed out just before the bomber exploded and crashed into the water.

Two days later, Rod caught and destroyed a 109 right over Luqa airfield. His score now stood at five destroyed enemy aircraft, officially making him an ace.

On October 14, a gunner put bullet holes in his aileron, and on the 15th, cannon and machine-gun fire from a marauding Messerschmitt riddled his Spitfire. Rod's first indication that an enemy was stalking him was when a bullet hole suddenly appeared in his left wing, followed by another about a foot out from the first. Within seconds, his engine exploded into a ball of fire. Without power and with a cockpit full of smoke, Rod slid the hood back and crawled out into space. Luckily, his parachute functioned, and he dropped into the Mediterranean. A rescue launch promptly fished him from the sea. As a result of this incident, he became a member of both the Caterpillar Club, instituted by the Irwin Parachute Company, for having to use his parachute to save his life (early parachutes were made of silk spun by caterpillars) and the Goldfish Club—gold for the value of life and fish for the sea, having survived a dunking.

Rod Smith also had to leave the cockpit temporarily in mid-November when he was felled by jaundice. Normally a fairly benign problem, Rod's illness, no doubt complicated by heat, dust, improper nourishment and high stress, was severe enough to warrant hospitalization. As soon as he recovered, he was sent back to England as a flying instructor at No. 53 Operational Training Unit in Hibaldston, Lincolnshire. On his arrival in January 1943, he learned that he had been awarded the Distinguished Flying Cross for having been:

> *"responsible for the destruction of six enemy aircraft since his arrival in Malta...This officer has always displayed the greatest determination and courage, and during the recent hard fighting has been an inspiration to all."*

He was invited to Buckingham Palace to receive his medal from King George VI.

On March 18, 1943, Rod was promoted to flight lieutenant. He had held the rank before, for only one month, until he fell ill in Malta and returned to England, where he reverted to flying officer. At the end of March, he was transferred to No. 55 Operational Training Unit in Annan, Dumfrieshire, Scotland, still on instructional duties. He returned to Acton Down in southern England for the fighter leader course in September.

Rod then went home to Canada on leave from October 24 to December 14. His family held an early Christmas that year because Rod had to return to duty in the UK on December 21.

Rod started 1944 with a posting to No. 401 (Ram) Squadron, based at Biggin Hill. He joined another Canadian, soon-to-be ace Flying Officer W.T. Klersy. The squadron was flying the newer Spitfire IXCs. The pilots flew fighter sweeps, rhubarbs, rangers and ramrods covering the Mosquitos bombing rocket emplacements. With No. 411 and 412 Squadrons, No. 401 Squadron formed part of No. 126 Wing.

On February 24 the wing's pilots were ordered airborne to meet American Flying Fortresses and their heavy escorts and bring them home from France. The sorties became monotonous because so many escorts were flying that the Luftwaffe wouldn't even consider rising to the challenge. Klersy scored a destroyed enemy aircraft during this time, but Smith never seemed to be flying when opportunity arose.

Rod Smith was posted to No. 412 Squadron on April 8 and entered a new phase of the air war. He was introduced to dive-bombing, using 500-pound bombs nestled under the Spitfire's fuselage. Adding to the pilots' anxiety was the minimal space between the bomb and the runway as the fighters taxied out for takeoff. A dive-bomber aimed the airplane at its target in a steep dive, and as the pilot pulled out of the dive, he was to release his bombs. They also had to calculate for forward travel of the ungainly bomb and the prevailing wind from the release point to the ground. There was no time for exacting calculations, so pilots usually counted to three or four before releasing the bombs. Of the 41 trips Rod flew in April and May, 18 were dive-bombing sorties.

The wing moved to Tangmere on the Sussex coast in preparation for the invasion of France. D-Day dawned with no sun below the overcast at 2000 feet. Visibility stayed at about five miles for the entire day. The Channel was choppy as the Allies' armada plunged toward the French coast. At daybreak, clouds of Spitfires, belching blue smoke, began their patrols over the beaches. Cold, wet and nauseated Allied troops stumbled ashore below them. The skies remained clear of Luftwaffe; any enemy aircraft that were sighted streaked for sanctuary before they could be engaged.

June 7 was an entirely different day as Junkers 88s returned to strafe the beaches. The flyers of No. 126 Wing had a field day, destroying 12 of the bombers near St. Aubin. But the German presence was short lived. The pilots' daily routine turned to uneventful dawn-to-dusk beach patrols.

The Allies' hastily constructed landing strips appeared near Crepon and Beny-sur-Mer, and on June 15, Spitfires moved in. That same day, the Luftwaffe fighters reappeared in force spoiling for a fight. The Canadians eagerly rose to meet them. That summer, No. 412 Squadron claimed 25 enemy aircraft destroyed but lost eight of their own. On July 7, in a dogfight over Argentan, Rod Smith raised his score to seven by destroying a Focke-Wulf 190.

The men were living in tents, often with trenches dug inside to avoid the hail of artillery shrapnel. Support staff worked wonders keeping the fighters, both men and machines, serviceable in the swirling dust that turned to sticky mud with each rainstorm. But morale remained high. They were doing what they had trained to do for years. Following the army's success, they began harassing the fleeing German ground forces. Enemy air activity was sporadic as Germany began to feel the pinch of fuel shortages, allowing the Canadian fighters to strafe anything that moved on the roads as well as communications facilities and supply dumps with little opposition.

The last weeks of September saw air combat intensify. The Luftwaffe targeted the bridges at Arnhem and Nijmegen in the Netherlands, and the Germans paid a heavy price for these incursions. On September 26, Flight Lieutenant Rod Smith was leading 12 Spitfires at 2000 feet near Nijmegen when he spotted two dozen Messerschmitt 109s below them just east of the bridge. Sailing in to attack, Rod chased one fighter for about two minutes before he got into firing position. His bullets struck the enemy's wing roots and fuselage. It began streaming glycol before it flipped over and crashed. Rejoining the swirling dogfighters,

Rod opened up on another Messerschmitt. His port cannon jammed, but instead of breaking off, Smith closed within spitting distance and fired again. The 109 exploded and hurtled downward. Fortunately, No. 412 Squadron suffered no losses, and an hour after landing, they were airborne again for another fight.

On September 27, the wing shot down more aircraft in one day than ever before. Nos. 411 and 412 Squadrons destroyed 22 enemy aircraft. Seven pilots from JG 26 were killed. Smith was again leading No. 412, and he again personally accounted for two Messerschmitt 109s. These raised his tally to 13 and were his last victories with 412. He was promoted to squadron leader and took command of No. 401 Squadron, flying from Le Culot, Belgium. His return was bitter-sweet. Familiar faces were gone; Bill Klersy completed his tour and left for England on September 16, and Hugh Trainor, who was the squadron's commanding officer, had been shot down. He bailed out but was made a prisoner of war on September 19.

Smith had an auspicious start with No. 401. On the first morning of his command, flying aircraft *MJ 448*, he led the squadron into a dogfight with more than 30 Messerschmitt 109s and Focke-Wulf 190s. Squadron Leader Smith destroyed two more 109s, making a total of six kills in three days

and earning a bar to his Distinguished Flying Cross.
Smith learned of the award on October 23:

> *"As squadron commander, this officer led 412
> Squadron on six missions in three days, during
> which period it destroyed 27 enemy aircraft and
> damaged nine others. This was accomplished during
> the enemy's persistent efforts to destroy bridges in the
> Arnhem and Nijmegen area which were vital to our
> ground forces."*

On October 5, three days after the 1st Gruppe
of JG26 shot down two 401 Squadron Spitfires
with no losses, the squadron scored a significant
first. Flying Spitfire *MK 577*, Smith led 12 aircraft
on a patrol over Nijmegen. A Messerschmitt 262
jet dove toward the bridge, and the Canadian
squadron promptly followed. During the chase,
five fliers shot at the enemy. The Messerschmitt
finally started to burn in the air and then crashed
in Allied territory. It was the first jet fighter to be
destroyed by pilots in either the RCAF or the RAF.

The squadron was now in the Netherlands,
living in the loft of a barn and making pilgrimages
to the nearest town for baths.

On November 22, Squadron Leader Smith led the
funeral cortege for Leading Aircraftsman Joe Butler,
who was killed when a landing Tempest caught
a gust of wind and chewed into the tail of a Spitfire.
Butler was riding on the tail—a common practice to
hold the Spit's tailplane down during taxiing.

On November 24, Smith had completed two tours, and Squadron Leader Everard replaced him. By the new year, he was back in Canada after flying 225 combat sorties over the previous year. He bounced from Winnipeg to Saskatoon to Regina, where he was released from active service on June 6, 1945.

In 1946, Rod Smith joined the RCAF Auxiliary and continued to fly with No. 401 Squadron in Montréal while he studied engineering at McGill University. He graduated in 1950 and moved to Toronto to study law at Osgoode Hall. Rod was promoted to wing commander and became the commanding officer of No. 411 Air Reserve Squadron. In 1952, he walked in front of a jet engine and suffered severe hearing loss that forced him to retire from the air force. Rod graduated as a lawyer in 1953 and moved to Vancouver, where he set up a very successful practice. He sustained his interest in aviation by flying small single-engine aircraft.

Rod Smith was a tall, handsome man who was never at a loss for female companionship, but he never married. He retired from his law practice in 1987 and traveled to Malta, Normandy and Germany, where he befriended Heinz Heuser, a pilot he had shot down over Malta in 1942. Rod Smith died in Vancouver on April 16, 2002, at 80 years old.

CHAPTER THIRTEEN

George Urquhart Hill
Scrapper Extraordinaire
(1918–1969)

WISPS OF SNOW CURLED IN A GUSTY WIND AS THE two-coach local train puffed into Pictou, Nova Scotia, on a cold November night in 1943. Crowds of men, some veterans of World War I, as well as women, starry-eyed teens and whooping children, impatiently waited to greet the only disembarking passenger. Squadron Leader George Hill was home on leave from the war.

Since George had left, in the autumn of 1939, the town had doubled in size and become a flourishing shipyard. He was home to savour his grandmother Arthur's cooking and enjoy a reunion with his mother, a high school principal in nearby Shubenacadie, and his brother, wireless air gunner Flight Sergeant Lloyd Hill, who was waiting in Halifax for a ship to take him overseas. But most of all he was home to marry his sweetheart, a girl he had courted while both attended Mount Allison University in Sackville, New Brunswick. Thelma Sanson married George in Moncton. The couple honeymooned in Ottawa courtesy of the Royal Canadian Air Force and the government of Canada before George returned to his flying duties in England.

George was born in Antigonish, Nova Scotia, the closest town with a hospital, on October 29, 1918. His early education was at Pictou Academy, where he made his mark as an exceptional student. He topped his class academically, winning the gold medal for the highest graduation exam marks and the Judge Patterson scholarship to Mount Allison for the year's highest aggregate marks. His classmates chose him to deliver the valedictory address at Pictou Academy's graduation exercises.

George was also popular for his athletic talents. He was a keen sailor in the Pictou Yacht Club, an excellent swimmer and diver and a skillful hockey player. Although he was of small stature, or maybe because of it, he was about the handiest boy with his fists in the town of 4000. In university, he held the intercollegiate featherweight boxing title for the Maritimes. As well, he played varsity hockey and rugby. George graduated with his Bachelor of Arts from Mount Allison and completed his pre-med courses. Inspired by his family doctor, Dr. Melton Young, and his son, Dr. Clarence Young, George hoped to study medicine at Dalhousie University in Halifax. Lack of funds hindered his ambition, and the outbreak of war changed his plans completely.

Squadron Leader George U. Hill, DFC and two Bars. In true fighter pilot tradition, the top button of his tunic is unfastened.

During George's last year at Mount Allison, in the spring of 1939, his friend Russ Johnson visited, full of tales of his exciting adventures in the RCAF. When it became obvious that war was imminent, George applied to the Canadian air force and was accepted. He enrolled in Halifax on

September 11, 1939. On September 4, the whole
air force, including auxiliary and reserve units,
had been placed on active service. At the time,
there were barely 4000 airmen in service. On
September 10, Canada entered the war against
Hitler.

George Hill, as a university graduate, was commissioned as a provisional pilot officer and learned
to fly Tiger Moths at the Halifax Aero Club. Upon
completing his initial training, on November 6, he
went to RCAF Station Trenton, Ontario. He traded
his civilian clothing for an air force blue uniform,
learned the art of spit-and-polish, participated in
continuous physical exercise and suffered under
a drill sergeant who taught him the difference
between his right and left feet. George was transformed into a first-class pilot trainee. He was given
the regimental number of C1075, in an era when
officers were still numbered as they joined up.

George's next stop on the road to his wings
parade was Camp Borden, Ontario. Hill arrived on
December 10, 1939, a week before the final
British Commonwealth Air Training Plan agreement was signed. George took his intermediate
flight training at Borden, where he spent part of
each cold winter day flying and the rest in ground
school learning the theory of flight, navigation,
airmanship and engines. Small arms, rifle and
machine-gun instruction were also included. The
men studied basic military organization and

command and control as laid down in the "bible," *King's Rules and Orders*. Winter flying gear included fur "Teddy bear" suits worn over long white turtleneck sweaters and heavy overalls with fleece collars and a multitude of pockets. Winter flying boots were fleece lined and so large that the pilot wore his shoes inside. Long leather gauntlets with silk liners, helmets, goggles, scarves, kneepad calculators for navigation, watches and maps rounded out the kit.

Of course, flying was the first priority, and students were pressured to get as many hours in the air as possible. Only the most extreme weather would scrub flying. The students learned to fly the Harvard, and a trainee required about 25 hours before solo flight was even considered. George Hill successfully completed training on February 28, 1940, and received his wings. A fellow graduate was Russ Bannock, who went on to fly twin-engine aircraft, while George was sent to single-engine fighters. The provisional part of the rank was dropped when their wings were presented, and they became pilot officers. George stayed in Borden for advanced instruction, and on April 22, he went to Trenton for further training.

All the new pilots expected to be posted overseas to operational squadrons. Most had their hopes dashed when they were kept in Canada as instructors for the new Commonwealth Air Training Plan. George's first hint of the changed plans was in Trenton, where the teaching focused on producing instructors for the elementary flying schools. Hill became a specialist at the Air Navigation School. At Trenton, he was promoted to flying officer on April 20. He left Trenton on July 27, 1940, for No. 2 Service Flight Training School in Uplands. On November 6, he was posted to No. 4 Service Flight Training School in Saskatoon, Saskatchewan and then on January 2, 1941, to No. 9 Service Flight Training School in Summerside, PEI.

In Summerside, George was the chief navigation officer. He wrote weekly to the commanding officer arguing the value of transferring him overseas. While Hill cooled his heels, he learned aerobatics from Wing Commander Elmer Fullerton, a prewar pilot who was an expert in unconventional flying. George continued to hone his flying and navigation skills, building confidence that was worth every minute of training time, since he did not have to think about flying the machine and could concentrate on his shooting later in combat. In Summerside, George was promoted again, to flight lieutenant, on July 1, 1941. After 20 months of instructional duties, George finally went overseas. He departed from Halifax on January 7, 1942.

En route to his operational squadron, George trained on Spitfires at No. 52 Operational Training Unit in Aston Down, Gloucestershire. Although he arrived with 840 flying hours experience, he

still needed to become totally familiar with the
fighter he would fly in combat. George's first
squadron was No. 421 (Red Indian) Squadron,
based at Digby, Lincolnshire, newly formed on
April 9 as the 20th RCAF squadron formed overseas. The squadron flew Spitfire VBs in a day-
fighter role with No. 12 Group. George arrived on
April 14 to take up his duties as a flight commander. His commanding officer suggested that
he fly a few sorties with No. 411 Squadron to get
operational experience. On April 29, he flew a circus
sortie with 411 and then joined them for a couple of fighter sweeps on May 1. Both operations
were uneventful.

Air Vice Marshall Raymond Collishaw,
a Canadian air ace from World War I, was a fre-
quent visitor to Digby. In discussing shooting, he
advised George to forget about deflection shooting. Buzz Beurling was the only good deflection
shooter, and he had been born with the gift.
Collishaw told Hill he should pay more attention
to positioning himself as close as possible behind
his enemy and to save his ammunition for sure
shots. George put this advice into practice and
to good effect. On May 2, the squadron moved to
Fairwood Common in south Wales to be part of
No. 10 Group.

On June 11, 1942, George was transferred to
No. 453 (RAAF) Squadron. He only stayed with
the Australians in Drem, East Lothian, for two

months. On August 13, he returned to a Canadian squadron, No. 403 (Wolf), commanded by Squadron Leader L.S. Ford, at Catterick, Yorkshire.

On August 17, the squadron moved to Manston in southeast England in preparation to provide top cover for the raid on Dieppe. Led by Ford, the squadron's first patrol on August 19 was at daybreak, patrolling at 3000 feet over the landing ships. A trio of Focke-Wulf 190s dove on Hill's section but flew past without getting a decent shot at the Canadians. Hill and his wingman, Sergeant M.K. Fletcher (an American in the RCAF), followed the Germans. Two Focke-Wulfs broke away, and Hill began firing into the third. The enemy aircraft went into a loop, giving Fletcher a target for a quick deflection shot. Both Hill and Fletcher made several more firing passes, and Hill narrowly missed slamming into his opponent. Suddenly, flames appeared at the enemy's port wing root, and the wing broke off. The German aircraft spun straight into the water from 500 feet. The two 403 pilots shared the kill.

Another fighter dove on Fletcher, but when Hill swooped in to attack, the enemy had to break off. Both Spitfires were running low on fuel and had to return to England, but in less than two hours they were airborne again, with Hill leading Blue Section. Dieppe was in flames, and dense smoke rose to about 3000 feet. The pilots had been briefed that the battle had been lost and the troops were being withdrawn. Their job was to patrol the area at 3000 feet to protect the ships. About a dozen Focke-Wulf 190s dropped below the layer of thin cloud and smoke, not expecting the Spitfire air guard. The Germans were suddenly caught in a dogfight.

Hill fired a long burst just ahead of an enemy aircraft and, as he expected, the 190 flew into the stream of bullets. The Focke-Wulf began trailing a thin line of gray mist and smoke but disappeared into the clouds before Hill could dispatch it. George followed the stricken airplane, but on top of the cloud he saw no sign of the damaged plane. A different 190 was cruising into the overcast, and Hill began a chase. Every time the Canadian fired, the German rocked violently. Bullet hits flashed all along the enemy's fuselage. Heading inland, the 190 led Hill along a narrow valley, and although he could see smoke coming from the other plane, George punched his gun button for one last shot. Nothing happened—his guns were empty. The last place he wanted to be was over enemy territory defenceless and rapidly using up fuel. He quickly returned to the squadron airstrip.

At 1620 hours, the squadron was again over the flotilla guarding its return. Squadron mates got two more enemy aircraft, but none of the Germans engaged Hill's Spitfire. A fourth patrol in the evening proved equally uneventful. Hill's first success gave him a shared destroyed, one probably destroyed and one damaged.

Weeks passed with no more contact with the Luftwaffe. Restless and impetuous, George began agitating for a transfer to action in the Middle East. Ford was reluctant to lose a flight commander and one of his ablest pilots, but when Ford went on leave, George's friend P.T. O'Leary, as acting commanding officer, approved his request for the new posting.

Hill's last flight with No. 403 Squadron was an air search-and-rescue patrol on December 13. He located seven USAAF fliers floating in two dinghies five miles off the French coast. After directing a rescue launch to pick them up, he headed home with a tremendously satisfied feeling in his gut.

On December 15, George went to Gibraltar to await further instructions. Traveling through East Africa in January 1943, he arrived at Souk-el-Kemis, in northwestern Tunisia, on February 2 to join No. 111 (RAF) Squadron. He flew his first sortie on February 4, when his section scrambled to a patrol height of 24,000 feet. At altitude, they were bounced by 10 Messerschmitt 109s who proved to be, in George's words, "rotten shots too!" In the ensuing skirmish, Hill's wingman fired then spun away because only one of his cannons worked. George employed deflection shooting to damage two of the attacking enemy.

On February 23, the squadron escorted a flight of "Hurribombers"—Hurricanes flying in a dive-bombing role—on a strafing mission. The Hurries attacked the enemy column, leaving a truck in flames, when a 109 pounced on them. Hill dove toward the fighter, got it dead in his sights and let fly. The enemy aircraft crashed in flames. The next day, he and his number two, Sergeant F. Mellor, shared in the destruction of a Messerschmitt 109. The pilot bailed out at 500 feet. On February 28, Hill, Mellor and Sergeant Spranger all shared in finishing off a 109.

March was an interesting month for George. On the 4th, he was leading the flight on a high cover tactical reconnaissance sortie at 14,000 feet when they spotted some Junkers 87s below them at 9000 feet. A group of German fighters covered the bombers. Hill's section attacked the Junkers 87s, and George destroyed two of them and damaged a third. He later recalled, "It was a fighter pilot's dream. We had them cold, and although the action didn't last more than five minutes, it was hectic, believe me."

Just as he was peeling away his engine seized and died. The glycol tank had been hit, and he had run out of engine coolant. George's Spitfire lost power with a Stuka hard on his tail. Fortunately, the German's aim was off, and he sprayed the air behind Hill's plane. George glided towards friendly lines and made a great wheels down landing, much to the delight of the cheering troops. The infantrymen thought the display was a "wizard show."

On March 24, he was engaging a Messerschmitt 109 from astern when another Spitfire attacked George's plane, forcing him to break off the pursuit. He was "very annoyed, to say the least!"

George led his section on a low-level attack looking for targets of opportunity on April 5. The pilots found and shot up two motor torpedo boats in the Bay of Tunis and headed home at ground level. Three Messerschmitt 109s queued up behind Hill's plane to take shots at him. Wing Commander Gilroy turned back to help. Hill had turned to try to engage his attackers three times before Gilroy got there and had put a good burst into one, damaging it badly. The German pilot bailed out of his unmanageable airplane. Gilroy and Hill had a running battle with the remaining two for over 40 miles, turning to meet their attacks at least nine times. The enemy aircraft finally rolled away from the fight. By the time George returned to base his engine was running on fumes, and he landed with dry tanks.

If March was interesting, April was spectacular. After the fight on April 5, George Hill's score only grew. On April 10, he scored one Focke-Wulf 190 probably destroyed and one damaged; April 11, one Messerschmitt 109 damaged; April 12, two 109s damaged; April 20, one 109 probably destroyed and one damaged; April 21, one 109 destroyed; and April 23, one 109 destroyed.

On April 27, Flight Lieutenant George Hill
was awarded the Distinguished Flying Cross as
"...a skillful leader whose ability has been well in
evidence during recent operations. He has participated in many sorties and has destroyed four
enemy aircraft." The air force recognized his
leadership by giving him command of the
squadron and promoting him to squadron leader.
He was 25 years old.

On May 1, he led the squadron for his first time
on a sortie between Tunis and Pantelleria. George
shared the destruction of a Heinkel 111 bomber
with four other squadron pilots. Each flyer completed a firing run on the lumbering machine. That
afternoon, on their second sortie, the squadron
made a dashing attack into a hornet's nest of
20-plus Messerschmitt 110s. The squadron shot
down seven of the enemy. Hill got one kill and
shared in two more. On his first pass, George shot
the leader out of the sky with a satisfying explosion. The second pilot made a head-on attack, but
George barrel-rolled over him, came in behind and
fired at a range of 50 feet. The pilot bailed out, but
the gunner went down with the aircraft.

On May 6, George got his last victory over North
Africa when he bagged a Messerschmitt 109. On
the 13th, the Axis forces surrendered, and the air
war ceased in the African theatre.

The squadron flew to Malta on June 10 to prepare for the invasion of Sicily. George learned on

July 3 that he had been awarded a bar to his Distinguished Flying Cross, primarily for his actions on the afternoon of May 1. He was described as "a courageous and skilful fighter." That same day, in a dogfight with 20 Messerschmitts, George destroyed a 109 and then noticed a pilot drifting down dangling from his parachute. Thinking it was wingmate Frank Mellor, George barreled in to fly cover. He had to skid his aircraft often to avoid enemy machines and saw the parachute go into the sea. George learned later that the pilot he had covered was a 19-year-old Luftwaffe airman whose engine had seized due to oil trouble. Both sides of this air conflict had reported cases of pilots being shot when hanging in their parachutes.

On July 10, 1943, soldiers of the 1st Canadian Division waded ashore near the town of Pachino, Sicily. The invasion of Italy was on, and No. 111 Squadron was flying daily top cover. On the 12th, George began chasing what he thought was a Messerschmitt 109 and nearly collided with the other aircraft as he unexpectedly overran it. The plane turned out to be an old Macchi 200, which Hill promptly dispatched. As he was turning away from the destroyed aircraft, Allied gunners opened fire and hit him. He was forced to land, out of fuel and glycol, on a field at Pachino. Six Messerschmitt 109s strafed his position while the gunners watched in silence. Stomping to the gun position, Squadron Leader Hill tore a strip off the artillery major for having his gunners shoot at an ally but disregard an enemy. Hill's squadron had a few anxious hours when he failed to return, until they learned that he was forced down but safe behind British lines. Later in the day, he was picked up and flown back to base.

The next day, July 13, they were patrolling the beachhead at dawn when a Junkers 88 appeared in the morning mist. George swung in behind the enemy, and his hits flashed on the bomber's port engine. As Hill was sliding over to aim a stream at the starboard engine, the enemy gunner loosed a hail of bullets that found their mark. The enemy went down, its left wing ablaze and its crew taking to their parachutes, but Hill's propeller was hit, and his engine was vibrating violently. Again he force-landed at Pachino and was fired at by the same gun crew. After landing, he witnessed the major haranguing his crew for having missed Hill's plane. However, the ground troops had seen the dogfight and were able to confirm his kill.

Hurrying back to his Malta base, Hill smarted from having been shot down twice in two days. He took off again and settled the debt by destroying a Focke-Wulf 190 in a brief decisive battle. On August 20, George was relieved of command and posted to Middle East headquarters.

He returned to Canada for some well-deserved leave and fired off a radiogram to Thelma advising her to prepare for a wedding. On the way home via Britain, he learned that he had been awarded a second bar to his Distinguished Flying Cross:

"Squadron Leader Hill, as a fighter pilot, has displayed exceptional courage and determination. He has destroyed at least fourteen enemy aircraft including one by night [the Junkers 88 at dawn] *and damaged many others. During recent operations from Malta, he led his squadron with skill and resolution, personally destroying four enemy aircraft within a few days. On one occasion he remained alone despite repeated and persistent attacks from six Messerschmitt 109s to obtain assistance for a comrade who had been forced to leave his aircraft by parachute."*

When Squadron Leader Hill arrived in Canada, he had the distinction of being only the second RCAF airman to win the air force's highest flying honour three times.

After seven weeks at home, George flew back to the UK and took command of No. 441 (Silver Fox) Squadron, deployed overseas from coastal defence duties in Canada. He arrived at RAF Station Digby to whip the new squadron into operational readiness. On February 8, the Canadians were ready for action as part of Fighter Command's 2nd Tactical Air Force. By late March, the squadron joined combat as part of No. 144 Wing, flying Spitfire IXs. Their wiry, tousle-haired commanding officer was all of 26 years old.

The squadron flew fighter sweeps and escorted heavy bombers. On April 25, 1944, Hill led the squadron out early in the morning to cover the return of almost 300 USAAF Flying Fortresses from attacks on enemy airfields in France. At 12,000 feet, he and wingman Pilot Officer R.H. Sparling got in a skirmish with enemy fighters. Hill fired at a Focke-Wulf 190 and hit it near the cockpit. George had to leave the fight because his long-range fuel tank broke off, damaging his tailplane. The pilots were holding on to their auxiliary tanks because it was a long way home; normally, they were immediately dropped when combat appeared inevitable. Hill could not get his engine restarted on the main tank, and he glided earthward. His squadron mates saw the Focke-Wulf crash and the Spitfire force-land near Epernay. Hill leapt from the cockpit and ran into some nearby woods.

With the help of the French Resistance, George evaded capture for about a month and made his way toward the Franco-Spanish border. He and a partner were standing in a railway station when agents of the Gestapo apprehended them. The airmen had been betrayed, and because they were in civilian clothes the pair were treated as spies rather than captured airmen. The Gestapo took them to Paris and then to the most notorious of French jails—Fresnes—where captured British agents of the Special Operations Establishment (spies) and members of the Resistance were imprisoned.

When George was interrogated, he was accused of spying. When he refused to give any information, he was thrown into solitary confinement and fed only a bowl of thin soup and one slice of stale bread each day. The airmen were told they would be taken to a concentration camp and executed as spies. For no apparent reason, 17 prisoners, including the captured pilots, were taken to Weisbaden civilian jail, where they were all housed in a single vermin-ridden room. The same poor food and interrogations continued. They were promised that if they told the Germans what they wanted by way of military information, their rations would be doubled.

When Luftwaffe officials discovered that the Gestapo was holding airmen, they demanded the prisoners be turned over. George spent the rest of the war at Stalag Luft 1. The difference in conditions was dramatic. By the end of the month, George had regained 30 pounds.

North of the Stalag was a Luftwaffe training field. On September 27, 1944, George was outside when he heard the distinctive sound of Merlin engines. A lone Mosquito swooped in to the airfield's circuit, shot down two trainers, banked and was gone. Comparing notes at a reunion after the war, he learned that the Mosquito pilot had been his friend from basic training days, Russ Bannock. The advancing Russian army liberated the camp, and on May 14. 1945, George was back in England.

He arrived in Canada on June 1 and was released
from service on September 17. His confirmed final
score was 11⅘ destroyed, 3 probably destroyed
and 11 damaged, all in air-to-air combat.

Another Maritimer who was a guest of the
Luftwaffe at Stalag Luft I was Squadron Leader
Hugh Trainor, who had been captured after bailing
out on September 19, 1944. He too was liberated
in April 1945 and was back in England two days
ahead of George Hill. They returned to Canada
together on June 1, and George was released from
the RCAF on September 17.

George Hill took his bride to Halifax and
finally enrolled in Dalhousie University's medical school. He graduated in 1950 and eventually
set up practice as a general practitioner in
Orangeville, Ontario. He and Thelma raised 10
children and were active in the community.
George served on the school board, on the hospital board and on the executives of the Medical
Society and his local Legion branch. He established and built the New Democratic Party
organization around Orangeville and was its
candidate for provincial office in 1967 and fed-
eral office in 1968 but lost both times. He
enjoyed curling and flew his own private aircraft
for years. Throughout, he was known as a family physician who still made house calls and
refused treatment to no one.

On November 12, 1969, driving to a curling match, his car was struck by another vehicle, and Dr. George Hill was killed instantly. Thelma had predeceased him, a victim of cancer. George's body was taken home to Pictou, Nova Scotia, for burial. As his coffin was lowered, an Argus anti-submarine patrol bomber from RCAF Station Greenwood, Nova Scotia, made a low, slow pass. The four-engine aircraft throttled back and tipped its wings in salute to a gallant officer and gentleman.

Boys to Men

WHEN DO LITTLE BOYS BECOME MEN? MAYBE IT'S WHEN they receive their driver's licence and a small degree of independence at 16 or when they are old enough to vote at 18.

Most of the men in these stories lived lifetimes of stress and danger before their 21st birthday. They had killed, and some had been killed. Were they men? Not completely. They still acted like boys playing at being men. In 2005, the Year of the Veteran, all of these courageous men were between 82 and 85 years of age. But their memories were still fresh—swirling airplanes dragging contrails in the cold blue sky, the loneliness of flying through stygian night skies guided only by the pale light of stars and the comradeship of shared beer and cigarettes in a blacked-out English pub warmed by an open fire and heavy wool socks.

A total of 232,000 men and 17,000 women enlisted in the Royal Canadian Air Force during World War II. The nation suffered a total of about 42,000 deaths;17,130 died in air force service. Canada contributed 86 RCAF Squadrons to the

war effort, and 47 of them were deployed overseas. Several thousand more Canadians served in
Britain's Royal Air Force. Of all those who served,
only approximately 150 fighter pilots became aces.
It was a completely unofficial title, and our records
are woefully incomplete. No official tally was kept,
and it is only through squadron and unit diaries and
histories that any kind of record can be established.
Hugh Halliday has done the definitive research
and published his findings in his book *The Tumbling
Sky*. Without his work, today's writers would be
completely lost in the wilderness.

Halliday lists 154 pilots who are acknowledged
as RCAF aces of World War II. Of those, 43—
roughly one-third—did not survive, killed in
action or in wartime flying accidents. He also lists
24 observers and radar operators who flew in
intruder aircraft, without whom their pilots would
certainly have never achieved ace status. The
leader, with 13 kills, was Flight Lieutenant Pat
Bing, who flew with Moose Fumerton. And don't
forget the gunners who flew cold, cramped night
sorties with Bomber Command. Two of these
brave souls are in this volume.

Each of these young pilots had total control of
a 350-miles-per-hour fighter aircraft with no radar,
no autopilot and few electronic aids. Between the
pilot's chest and the engine sloshed 90 gallons of
high-octane fuel. He wore no crash helmet or
other protective clothing, just layers to keep warm.

He could unleash thirteen pounds of ammunition at the touch of a button after solving the sighting equation against his foe without becoming a target himself—with only three seconds in which to do it. He often flew at 30,000 feet with no cockpit heating or pressurization. Diving and twisting in dogfights, he endured up to six times the force of gravity before "G" suits had been invented, and he did not have an ejection seat, having to slide back the canopy, drop the side door and crawl out on the wing to escape. He was often only 19 years old.

By and large, these men were achievers. It took perseverance and determination just to continue their daily duty. For most, the same qualities ensured successful civilian careers. Many resumed their education where they left off, becoming engineers, lawyers, doctors and men of commerce. Some who left the farm returned, but most did not. The veterans took an entrepreneurial attitude into postwar life that paid good dividends. Some stayed in the air force, usually with a reduction in rank, and rose once more to senior positions in the service. With few exceptions these men built successful postwar careers with the same mettle that brought them wartime success.

They became builders, these boys of Canada, contributing their vision, constructed from the death and destruction witnessed during their teens, to the evolution of their nation into its prominent status on the world's stage. The deeds of these young fliers remain beacons of hope and progress for the current generation.

> *"He that outlives this day, and comes safe home,*
> *Will stand tip-toe when this day is nam'd."*

— Shakespeare, King Henry V

Glossary

Ammo – ammunition

ASR – Air-sea rescue

Bogey – unidentified radar contact

Bounce – take another aircraft unawares from higher altitude

CAN/RAF – Canadians in the RAF

Circus – short-range day-bombing operations with fighter escort. The object was to tempt the Luftwaffe fighters to engage the escorts and concentrate the enemy's resources in specific areas of the RAF's choosing

CO – Commanding Officer

Conspicuous Gallantry Medal – Royal Air Force medal awarded to airmen of non-commissioned rank for gallantry in air operations against the enemy

Distinguished Flying Cross – awarded to officers and warrant officers for acts of valour, courage, or devotion to duty performed while flying in active air operations against the enemy

Distinguished Flying Medal – awarded to non-commissioned officers and men in the air force with the same conditions as the DFC to officers

Ditch – to make a forced landing of an aircraft in water

Dispersal – widely separated areas around an airfield where aircraft are parked

Dogfight – confused air battle

Drogue target – A fabric cone or cylinder open at both ends, towed behind an aircraft as a target

Feather – to rotate the propeller blades in such a way as to lessen the air resistance

Fighter-bomber – an aircraft that serves as both a fighter plane and light bomber

Flak – enemy anti-aircraft fire, from German *flugzeugabwehrkanone*

Flower patrols – flown in support of Bomber Command raids and directed against German night-fighter bases

Forward field – an air base near the front lines

Gaggle – formation of aircraft

Glycol – engine coolant

Gong – medal

Gruppe – German fighter group

HMCS – His Majesty's Canadian Ship

HMS – His Majesty's Ship

HMT – His Majesty's Troopship

Intruder sorties – offensive flights into hostile air space to destroying enemy bombers at or near their bases

Jagdgeschwader – German fighter wing

Jadgkorps – a German fighter command grouping

Jerry – German

Kite – aircraft

Line astern formation – aircraft flying in a straight line behind the leading airplane

Luftwaffe – German Air Force

Mae West – inflatable life jacket with bulging front

Mahmoud flight – a radar-equipped Mosquito mission to intercept an enemy aircraft over Europe that was being tracked by ground radar in the United Kingdom

Mayday – distress signal, from French *m'aidez*

Nacelle – aircraft engine casing

Pancake – land

Pathfinders – elite squadrons of experienced airmen from the best crews who flew ahead of the bomber stream to precisely locate targets. They orbited and dropped flares for the bombers to home in on for accurate bombing

Perspex – an acrylic plastic windscreen, purportedly shatterproof

Petrol – gasoline

Piece of Cake – easy, a cinch

Probable – enemy aircraft probably destroyed

RAF – Royal Air Force

Ramrod – a short-range bomber raid to destroy a specific target

Ranger operation – a sortie by day or night when one or two aircraft would track down any target within range—trains, ships, vehicles, barracks, or aircraft

RCAF – Royal Canadian Air Force

RCN – Royal Canadian Navy

Rhubarb – low-level attack on ground targets of opportunity

Rodeo – fighter sweep

Roundel – a circular identifying mark, usually in the colours of a country's flag. The RAF roundel has a red centre with concentric circles of white and blue. The RCAF roundel is similar, but has a red maple leaf in the centre

Scramble – quick take-off

Serrate operation – when radar-equipped Mosquitos went out searching for enemy night fighters in the bomber stream

Sortie – operational flight

Staffel – German squadron

Sweep – offensive fighter patrol to draw in enemy fighters

USAAF – United States Army Air Force

USAF – United States Air Force

V-1 – buzz-bomb; German robot bomb

V-2 – German artillery rocket

Winco – airmen's affectionate slang term for a Wing Commander

Notes on Sources

Bashow, David L. *All The Fine Young Eagles*, Toronto: Stoddart Publishing Co. Ltd., 1996.

Bishop, Arthur. *The Splendid Hundred*, Toronto: McGraw-Hill Ryerson, 1994.

Bottomley, Capt. Nora. *424 Squadron History*, Belleville, ON: The Hangar Bookshelf, 1985.

Bracken, Robert. *Spitfire: The Canadians*, Erin, ON: Boston Mills Press, 1995

Bracken, Robert. *Spitfire II: The Canadians*, Erin, ON: Boston Mills Press, 1999.

Caldwell, Donald L. *JG 26: Top Guns of the Luftwaffe*, New York: Ivy Books, 1991.

Coughlin, Tom. *The Dangerous Sky: Canadian Airmen in World War II*, Toronto: The Ryerson Press, 1968.

Deighton. Len. *Fighter, The True Story of The Battle of Britain*, London: Random House, 1977.

Gordon, John. *...Of Men and Planes, Volume II*, Ottawa, Love Printing Service Ltd., 1968.

Hawthorn, Tom. "Pilot shot down five enemy planes in four days," *The Globe and Mail*, Toronto: August 2, 2004.

Hovey, Capt. Richard H. and Capt. Don Schmidt. *416 Squadron*, Chatham, NB: 1974.

Liddell Hart, Sir Basil H. *History of the Second World War*, New York: G.P. Putman's Sons, 1970.

MacFarlane, John & Robbie Hughes. *Canada's Naval Aviators*, Shearwater, Nova Scotia: The Shearwater Aviation Museum Foundation, 1997.

Marion, Normand, editor. *Camp Borden, Birthplace of the RCAF*, Borden, ON: 16 Wing, 1999.

McCaffery, Dan. *Air Aces*, Toronto: James Lorimer & Company, 1990

Middlebrook, Martin and Chris Everitt. *The Bomber Command War Diaries*, New York: Viking Penguin Inc., 1985.

Milberry, Larry. *Canada's Air Force At War and Peace, Volume One*, Toronto: CANAV Books, 2000.

Milberry, Larry. *Canada's Air Force At War and Peace, Volume Two*, Toronto: CANAV Books, 2000.

The Canadians at War 1939/45, Volume 1, Montréal: The Reader's Digest, 1969.

The Canadians at War 1939/45, Volume 2, Montréal: The Reader's Digest, 1969.

Milberry, Larry and Hugh Halliday. *The Royal Canadian Air Force: At War 1939 – 1945*, Toronto: CANAV Books, 1990.

McIntosh, Dave (ed). *High Blue Battle, The War Diary of No. 1 (401) Fighter Squadron, RCAF*, Toronto: Stoddart Publishing Co. Ltd., 1990.

Nijboer, Donald. *Gunner: An Illustrated History of World War II Aircraft Turrets and Gun Positions*, Erin, ON: Boston Mills Press, 2001.

Nolan, Brian. *Hero, The Buzz Beurling Story*, Markham, ON: Penguin Books, 1983.

Price, Alfred. *Spitfire, A Complete Fighting History*, London: The Promotional Reprint Company Ltd., 1991.

Ralph, Wayne. *Aces, Warriors & Wingmen, Firsthand Accounts of Canada's Fighter Pilots in the Second Word War*, Mississauga, ON: John Wiley & Sons Canada Ltd., 2005.

Roberts, Leslie. *There Shall Be Wings: A History of The Royal Canadian Air Force*, Toronto: Clarke, Irwin & Company Limited, 1959.

Shores, Christopher. *Air Aces*, Greenwich, CT: Bison Books Corp., 1981.

Shores, Christopher. *Duel For The Sky*, Garden City, NY: Doubleday & Company, 1985.

Shores, Christopher. *History of the Royal Canadian Air Force*, Greenwich: Bison Books Corp., 1984.

Soward, Stuart E. *Hands To Flying Stations, Volume 1*, Victoria, BC: Neptune Developments (1984), 1993.

Soward, Stuart E. *Hand To Flying Stations, Volume II*, Victoria, BC: Neptune Developments (1984), 1995.

Soward, Stuart E. *A Formidable Hero*, Victoria BC: Trafford, 2003.

Sturtivant, Ray. *British Naval Aviation, The Fleet Air Arm, 1917-1990*, London: Arms & Armour Press Ltd., 1990.

Sturtivant, Ray & Theo Balance. *The Squadrons of the Fleet Air Arm*, Tunbridge, Kent: Air Britain (Historians) Ltd., 1994.

Taprail Dorling "Taffrail", Captain H. *Ribbons and Medals*, Liverpool: Philip, Son and Nephew, Ltd. 1956.

Townsend, Peter. *Duel of Eagles*, New York: Simon and Shuster, 1970.

421 Squadron History, Stittsville, ON: Canada's Wings Inc., 1982.

424 Squadron History, Belleville, ON: the Hangar Bookshelf, 1985.

Index

Larry Gray

Larry Gray is a retired member of the Canadian Armed Forces. He served as a radio officer, air navigator and information officer before becoming the managing editor for the newspaper of the Canadian Army in Europe. He has also been a United Nations military observer and served as part of the Commonwealth Election Team in Zimbabwe in 1980. After he retired from the RCAF, he served with the Royal Canadian Legion, the Veterans Review and Appeal Board, and the Office of the National Defence and Canadian Forces Ombudsman.

Gray has received the Minister of Veterans Affairs Commendation, the Queen's Jubilee Medal, the United Nations Peacekeeping Medal, the Canada Celebration 88 Medal for Voluntarism, the United Nations Service Medal and the Canadian Forces Decoration. He has published several articles on World War I in *Esprit de Corps* magazine and has written two books on the war dead of Carleton Place, Ontario: *We Are the Dead* and *Fathers, Brothers, and Sons*.

Here are more titles from
FOLKLORE PUBLISHING...

BILLIONAIRES OF CANADA
Their Stories and their Influence on Canada
by Tim le Riche
From the Bronfmans who built their Seagrams empire during Prohibition to the McCains who started out as small potatoes but wound up the world's largest manufacturer of french fries, read these fascinating stories and many more.
$9.95 CDN • ISBN10: 1-894864-56-5 • ISBN13: 978-1-894864-56-5 • 5.25" x 8.25" • 168 pages

GREAT CANADIAN ROMANCES
Love, Scandal, Deceit and Passion
by Barbara Smith
The stormy romance of Pierre Elliot Trudeau and Margaret Sinclair, the murderous pairing of James and Johannah Donnelly and the on-ice sparks between Jamie Sale and David Pelletier are some of the legendary Canadian love stories in this book full of passionate, tragic and bizarre tales.
$9.95 CDN • ISBN10: 1-894864-52-2 • ISBN13: 978-1-894864-52-7 • 5.25" x 8.25" • 144 pages

GREAT CANADIANS
Twelve Profiles of Extraordinary People
by Angela Murphy
This book pays tribute to just a few of the many people whose contributions to Canada are unique. From environmentalists to politicians, from sports figures to writers, these men and women exemplify what it means to be Canadian. Read about Tommy Douglas, David Suzuki, Terry Fox, Margaret Artwood and many more.
$9.95 CDN • ISBN10: 1-894864-46-8 • ISBN13: 978-1-894864-46-6 • 5.25" x 8.25" • 144 pages

RENEGADE WOMEN OF CANADA
The Wild, Outrageous, Daring and Bold
by Marina Michaelides
A collection of stories about fascinating Canadian women who never followed the rules. Among those featured are rebellious songstress, k.d. lang; Naomi Klein, journalist, author and anti-globalization activist; Nell Shipman, silent film actress, producer and director who did her own stunts and was the first woman ever to do a nude scene in *Back to God's Country*, the most successful Canadian silent film ever made; and Manon Rheaume, the first woman to play in the NHL.
$9.95 CDN • ISBN10: 1-894864-49-2 • ISBN13: 978-1-894864-49-7 • 5.25" x 8.25" • 168 pages

PIONEER CANADIAN ACTORS
The Stories Behind Legends of the Silver Screen
by Stone Wallace
This book celebrates the Canadian men and women who showed the world that some of the most impressive acting talent comes from Canada. Learn about the careers of Donald Sutherland, Lorne Greene, Christopher Plummer, Mary Pickford, William Shatner and more.
$9.95 CDN • ISBN10: 1-894864-42-5 • ISBN13: 978-1-894864-42-8 • 5.25" x 8.25" • 144 pages

Look for these and other books from Folklore Publishing at your local bookseller and newsstand or contact the distributor, Lone Pine Publishing, directly.
In the U.S. call 1-800-518-3541.   In Canada, call 1-800-661-9017.